To: Candy

THE CORRIDOR THAT LIES
BETWEEN GREATNESS & INSANITY

Lorenzo Hogans

Enjoy the book! Try to be a blessing to someone whenever you can. You've already been a blessing to me and I pray this very book is a blessing to YOU.

The Imperfect Messenger

THE CORRIDOR
THAT LIES BETWEEN
GREATNESS & INSANITY

Lorenzo Hogans II

ISBN: 0996397507
ISBN 13: 9780996397506

CONTENTS

PROLOGUE

THIS BOOK SERVES AS A song of redemption for those who are waiting to be redeemed. There is wonderful splendor encoded in the very strands of your DNA that is waiting to awaken. Many of us know that it's there and that it exists within us, but a tremendous number of humans in general cannot seem to tap into the pinnacle of their greatness. Some have seen flashes and the traces that those flashes leave in their lives as by-products. True greatness is achieved when and only when we ask for it from the Creator of all things. The good news is that God is waiting right now to grant it to you this very second—but there's more. It takes a special individual to maintain this gift because it is not always "roses and butterflies" when you travel this path. As the phrase goes, this path is the path less traveled, making it a little more difficult to stay the course than the average route. The greatness that I speak of that God is waiting intently to grant you, if you haven't already guessed it, is the gift of eternal life or salvation in Jesus Christ, God's son. However, there is a corridor that lies between his greatness and your insanity. This corridor is a pit.

This corridor is a vacuum. Think of it as a vortex, a black hole that is relentless in holding you in its grasp of confusion and aggravation. The good news is that you can successfully escape this vexing bondage when you get ready, only you cannot do it alone. I personally realized that I could not succeed alone in the midst of devastating failure that left me heartbroken, depressed, and greatly confused about my purpose. This is a true story of tribulations followed by successful efforts to strengthen my confidence in God. I never was in disbelief but yearned for signs from God to aid me in my darkest of times. Walk with me through what I have termed "the corridor," where I reveal life lessons that were learned in my spiritual journey to help sustain your faith when even you possibly get caught in a similar mental state. There is a God.

CHAPTER 1
SALVATION

As a working paramedic, I have been privileged to make a difference in the lives of the sick and injured. On a frequent basis, my eyes have the opportunity to see and help those in their darkest hours. Most of the time, no one has prepared for this hour to come simply because people don't expect tragedies to happen to *them*. These people did not expect these unfortunate occurrences to take place in their lives at that particular moment. Therefore, they are caught in a vulnerable state that requires a helping hand to see them through. Fortunately for patients who come to this event in their lives, be it a medical or trauma emergency, society has put into effect a safety net. This safety net is called emergency medical services. Emergency medical services comprise EMTs, paramedics, and firefighters who may be dual certified in both firefighting and medical training. As you may imagine, some of these emergency calls are more severe than others. One emergency call may require stabilization, such as a simple ice pack for minor swelling, while another emergency call may demand lifesaving CPR efforts coupled with strong resuscitative medication. The one thing that all emergency calls irrefutably have in common is the need for help. In other words, vulnerability has suddenly risen into the forefront of someone's life, and that person needs assistance.

Life has a way of throwing us curveballs unexpectedly. I'll be the first one to tell you that it's not fair. Life has never been fair, as a matter of fact, but we can't get pulled into the time-wasting act of griping and moaning about what hand we were dealt. What we can do is dictate how to respond with a positive mental attitude and consultation with our Lord and savior, Jesus Christ, through prayer. God wants the best for us; he does not always give those of us that believe in him what we want, but with faith and fervent prayer, you can expect him to provide what you need. Wouldn't it be grand if you had a father that would give you all that you need? Jesus Christ's Father, the one and only Lord of all the world, wants to be that father to you. Like people in their darkest hour during an emergency 911 call, we all need assistance in one way or another. Many of us have needed assistance in multiple areas all at the same time! This life is not meant to be lived without assistance, whether the assistance is spiritual or nonspiritual. Preparation is the key for surviving disaster. Taking the appropriate measures to prepare for turmoil is the sure way to deal with catastrophe appropriately. Tomorrow is never promised, and the next few moments of your life are never guaranteed. I have seen death and held it in my arms.

Though I ponder many questions in dealing with death on emergency calls, the most prominent question that lingers in my mind is the question of salvation in that particular patient's life. Did this person believe in God? Did this person accept Jesus Christ into his or her heart as Lord and savior? And further, did this person realize all that God had planned for him or her while on this earth? The fact of the matter is that life is short. Life is extremely short in relation to eternity, so it is imperative that we become saved so that our souls are preserved in the Book of Life when God reviews it on Judgment Day. Life is interesting, to say the least; we are born into it with a relatively random hand that we're dealt, challenged to make do with what we have been given for a short time, and then boom—all of a sudden our final day has come.

Since I graduated high school, which today was only six years ago, I can recall three individuals who unexpectedly passed away. One man I used to play pickup basketball with downtown ended up having an undisclosed heart condition that suddenly swept him off of this earth with no warning or phone call in advance. Death did not say to my buddy from high school, "Here I come; I hope you're ready for me!" Another of my friends from high school was murdered. This particular young man actually played on my very first soccer team as a child. Little did either of us know that he would be taking an early exit from life by way of a homicide. The final high school student was a mere acquaintance that shared a senior English class with me. She was very quiet and reserved. This particular young woman just recently underwent a fatal vehicle accident. The article read that she was making a left turn and was T-boned.

Now I have only been out of high school for six years, and already three individuals of my acquaintance have lost their lives. All three of these incidents left the victims' family and friends devastated and in a state of utter sorrow. These families loved their children very much. I attended one of the funerals, and the mourning I witnessed from the families was unnerving. Death has become a common theme in my life due to my line of work and the way life unfolds on its own. The message I'm extending to the reader is the message of salvation. Salvation is the universal preparation for death. For all people are created to last forever. The stipulation regarding this truth is that you ask for this gift of eternal life by surrendering your life out of the love in your hearts because Jesus Christ died for your sins. Sin is a universal weakness that we all have in common. The only person who is completely blameless and perfect, never having sinned once, was Jesus Christ. Therefore, he was worthy in the eyes of God to be made a sacrifice for the sins of all men. God knew that we would not be perfect, so he sent his only Son to make sure we had a savior to literally save us from sin. The second part to asking for this eternal gift of life through God's Son, Jesus Christ, is that we repent of our sins wholeheartedly. I say *wholeheartedly* because true forgiveness is only granted when you are truly sorrowful and desire to perform better, purer actions thereafter.

The beauty in repentance is not only the gift of eternal life, but it is also the inheritance of God's fatherly counsel and blessing while here on earth! The apostle Paul, who was a devout sinner turned strong Christian man, wrote that we should put to death our earthly nature, including "things such as sexual impurity, lust, evil desires, and greed, which is idolatry" (Col 3:5). The apostle Paul also writes to us that we should put off our old self (sinful self), which belongs to our former lives, and put on our new self, created after the likeness of God in true righteousness and holiness (Eph 4:22–24). This means that our old ways of doing things before we accepted Jesus Christ into our lives were not acceptable, hence the purpose of repenting. We must renew our minds with the help of God and pray for strength to walk upright in God's holy righteousness. Repentance requires humility and the identification that you are indeed a sinner that needs to be forgiven. We can be glad that repentance is available to us through the grace of God because sin is a universal disease that we all have and will have for our entire lives. Forgiveness of our sins is God's way of telling us that he knows we're not perfect and never will be. All of us would be doomed had it not been for God's glorious grace. I thank him frequently that he is so gracious to such a sinful people. Imagine if you could never be given a second chance to get things right. This expectation is quite preposterous because we all make mistakes. God knows that we are all creatures of failure that will never measure up to his undying love. He loves us through and through, no matter what. This is not to say that Christians are to use salvation as a "get out of jail free" card and meanwhile continue living in sin with ruthless intentions. That would be toying with God, and woe to anyone who intentionally thinks he or she can out-smart God. Salvation is why Christians can be glad under any circumstance.

Life has its ups and downs, but when it's all said and done, glory will be given to Jesus Christ the King as well as to his children—those of us that have chosen to believe in him. Jesus was an intriguing person in all that he did during his time on earth. Many did not know just what to think of him, for he did not have any apparent discretion for the company he surround-ed himself with. Here you have a perfectly sinless man walking the earth who did not mind being in the company of very sinful individuals—and not just discreetly sinful people but offensively sinful people such as thieves and street harlots. The underlying purpose for this was revealed by Jesus when he addressed this concern with an enlightening answer to the masses. Jesus ex-claimed that it is not the healthy who need a doctor, but the sick (Lk 5:31). The message I'm extending to the reader is that it does not matter where you come from or what you've done. Jesus is forgiving of everyone, sinners of every category! All you have to do is be willing to accept Jesus into your life and actively put forth an honest effort to be more like him. Everyone has his or her own perspective on going to church, but it is always rather humorous when a person is asked or invited to attend church and he or she replies with, "I'm not good enough—God doesn't want people like me in his church." This is just not true, and I'm here to tell you that you will never be too sinful to repent or simply attend church. God rejoices when sinners of all sorts come to him for knowledge and learning. God does not only want the most mature of Christians to attend church and learn about his teachings, but also the lost and the hurt and the sinners in need of repentance. That was the epitome of what he told everyone when people questioned his company. Don't ever let the thoughts of what you have done keep you from God's temple or family in Christ. He longs to see each and every one of us to come to the startling conclusion that we need him and can't make it without him. Having read the Bible in its entirety, I know this proclamation to be true because throughout the Bible is a long list of imperfect sinners that relied on Jesus Christ as their Lord and savior for their strength because of the fact that they were so prone to sin.

There's something called a person's carnal nature that will be discussed later in this book that entails the characteristics of that corridor reflected in all of us. This carnal nature is what we were born with and how we were all manufactured. God manufactured us this way, and he's completely aware of our flaws. In noting this, we can all have confidence that he accepts us no matter what our pasts have been. Our decisions from our past will not be held against us so long as we repent wholeheartedly. I think about the world and all its evil on a regular basis and shake my head at some of the brainless chaos that goes on in the workplace, out in public, and even in the church. It's such an imperfect world that we live in that we must take the time to evaluate preparatory measures that require action.

Atop that list should be establishing a relationship with God. To establish a relationship with God, you must first repent of your sins, as I have mentioned already, and continually model yourself after Jesus Christ. The world has many lovers of self who are only interested in self-advancement, self-image, self-righteousness, and the overall glorification of self. As Christians we must lead lives of servant leadership, a selfless life that mirrors Jesus's life to the best of our abilities; this is what being a Christian is all about. By modeling ourselves after Christ, we inadvertently draw closer to him in our relationship with him.

Please avoid getting caught up in the foolishness of thinking that the Christian life is one of boredom and monotony. The Christian way of living is one of supernatural blessings and reward! For there is none other than God who can grant you the ultimate gift of eternal life; therefore you should rejoice to know such a gracious God. That he cares about sinners is a blessing in itself! God loves you so much. He loves you more than anyone else loves you or ever will love you. If you think about the measures he took to give you eternal life, it is mind-boggling. Essentially, what God did was take his only Son and give him to be sacrificed for all of us. Those of you who have children can identify with the love that is present from parents toward their children. If you were to be asked to give up your daughter or son as a sacrifice, the likelihood of that not being a devastating decision is very low. Not to mention, if that daughter or son were your only child, how much greater of an evaluation would you have to make? In probably the most famous verse in the Bible, John the disciple writes of God's sacrifice for you (Jn 3:16). Won't you trust in a love that deep? This is no ordinary love; this is not love that flails in the wind like a plant with no roots. This love is an undying love that will always be there for you in any situation or obstacle life presents to you. There will be times when things you don't understand happen to you, and you're left wondering, why me? There will be times of tragedy, distress, and chaotic turmoil that leave you battered and bruised with seemingly no one in sight.

There will even be times of brokenheartedness coupled with damaged emotions producing permanent scars. In these darkest of times, we must already be prepared with the mental capacity and fervent prayer in order to deal with the devastation without giving up all hope. A cousin of mine lost her five-month-old baby. Devastation and emotional wreckage came to her unexpectedly. She didn't ask for this to happen to her, nor did she ever plan for her child to suddenly die. In times of distress, it is important that we continually give thanks to God because it shows spiritual maturity, and this makes God elated to see his children becoming more mature. If we complain and harden our hearts toward God, it will not expedite us receiving the blessings God wants to shed on our lives for obeying and trusting in him.

A great example of this story is the story of Job. In the Bible, there was a servant of the Lord who was tested profoundly. Job had it all. He had everything the average man would want, typically speaking. Job had wealth, he had a family, and he had health. Satan wanted to test his faithfulness, so he asked God to take away those blessings from Job to effectively measure whether Job was a fair-weather friend or not. Job did not disappoint the Lord. God took away all his wealth and abundance of livestock and then was pleased when Job remained faithful. Satan, disappointed and ridiculed, asked God to take away Job's family in order to see if Job would still remain faithful to God. So Job lost his family, his children, and his house, but his wife was kept alive. Again Job remained faithful in his trust in the Word of God. Satan, baffled at Job's tenacity, spoke with God yet another time and asked God to take away Job's health. God approved this request but did not allow Satan to kill Job. Job met his darkest of hours as he lay down in a sickly state with boils on his skin. His three good friends came to mourn with him and be supportive but ended up pointing the finger at him for all of the misfortune! They placed the blame on Job for his state and essentially became more of a burden to their good friend Job when he needed uplifting. In the end, God blessed Job for not hardening his heart and continuing to trust in the Lord. The Lord must have been elated by Job's perseverance because he gave him back everything that was taken away from him—and then some! The story of Job's faithfulness is such a great example because this was a guy who "got" it. He understood completely that it was not about himself but about God's will. Therefore, God rewarded Job for all of his faithfulness because he was proud of him like a father is proud of his son.

How devastating would it be to have been in the shoes of Job? Do you have the desire and the guts to trust in God, even in the worst of times? As I previously disclosed, this path of following God reaps many blessings, but the path itself is not always the prettiest of paths. In the event of disappointment or unsure results and outcomes, believers must not falter, for God knows exactly what he is doing. We do not always know just what God is thinking or doing, but the Bible says that all things work for good for those that believe in him. God is sculpting a plan for our lives that may not be available to our understanding at the given time, though it is definitely for our best.

THE POTTER AND THE SINGER

At my local church, there was a couple who came to pass along their powerful testimony that their salvation in Christ had produced. This couple was undoubtedly an original pair; they each had unique personalities. The gentleman had been a successful businessman on Wall Street making the big bucks. He explained that at the time, he felt that he had everything anyone could ever want. His nice Lamborghini was a dream car. His job on Wall Street was one of great merit, and to put the icing on the cake, he was married to a beautiful young woman. His wife then gave the church an overview of her past lifestyle as a Broadway performer. She too during that time in her life felt as though she had obtained everything she ever wanted. She got to dress up and be beautiful for many to admire and be entertained via her Broadway performances. The married couple even told the church the manner in which they got married, which was startling. They explained that they both made an emotionally charged decision to get married within a matter of months, traveled to Las Vegas, and tied the knot. The repercussions of this frantic commitment to marriage resulted in many bouts of rage. The married couple claimed that the verbal abuse between the two of them was relentless. They both came to the conclusion that something vital was missing in their lives. This void that seemed to be simultaneously affecting both of their lives was filled by the acceptance of Jesus Christ.

The two went on to tell in detail how accepting Jesus Christ into their lives had been the best decision they ever made. It also changed the course of their decisions. The husband explained to us how he was touched by the Lord and began to use his favorite hobby as a ministry to touch the lives of others who were experiencing that same void in their lives. His favorite hobby was none other than pottery. His wife professed the same in deciding to use her hobby to reach the lives of the lost, as she once was. Her hobby was singing, and as a personal witness, she was indeed a talented singer.

The husband was spectacular in his craft as well. On the stage he had a large potter's wheel that rotated as he sculpted a ball of clay. As his hands were busy sculpting this gigantic ball of clay, he told his and his wife's story of salvation. In detail, he told of how drastically making the decision to be a follower of Christ had directly affected his life's course of direction. His enthusiasm was captivating, as well as his wife's singing, which supported the message and set the tone of their delivery. Suddenly, the husband took his fist and smashed the beautiful vase that he was sculpting! The entire congregation gasped in disbelief, for the wonderful piece of artwork was now ruined. He cleared his throat and proceeded to tell the church that they needed to relax and calm down. He calmly declared to us that he had other plans for the clay. His words were, "Every performance my wife and I have, when I smash the clay, we get the same response... And it's because you all thought I was making a vase, when my plans were to make a bowl." Immediately the crowd let out a sigh of relief and cheerful laughter. The potter used this illustration to reveal the way that God works in a believer's life for his own purposes. The message of the potter's and his wife's performance was to relay the importance in believing in Jesus Christ, even when things aren't exactly how we may feel they should be at the given time. God has plans for us all beyond what we can see sometimes. You may be thinking one thing while God is smiling and creating another outcome greater than what you have planned. When you choose to envelop yourself in God's love, it is important to understand this concept because there will be moments where doubt may creep into the mind.

You'll Need to Surrender

Salvation could not be mentioned in its entirety without mentioning the vitality of surrender. The control desired in the lives of many to know what's going to happen next is very common. If we all pretty much know what will come of our lives, then life can throw us a lot fewer monkey wrenches in the midst of what we have planned, right? Wrong. Another area of life that consumes a vast portion of our decisions is that of gratification. We all desire to be pleased in one way or another, which alters the very decisions that we all make. The process is typically carried out in this fashion: if happiness seems to be the result of our decision, then we indeed make it. If pain or any kind of inconvenience seems to be the outcome of a decision, then we look for another option. Surrendering to Jesus Christ is to make that decision that may not be what we want in our everyday lives because we trust that he loves us and wants the best for our lives. Surrender is to deny oneself for the will of God rather than the imperfect will that we desire for ourselves from our own imperfect minds.

The story, or Gospel, of Jesus Christ has four different accounts. *Gospel* simply means "good news." The four Gospels each had four different authors that give their own personal account of Jesus's life. These four Gospels, Matthew, Mark, Luke, and John, all tell the same story with small discrepancies. When Jesus lived, there along with him were twelve disciples. In Luke,

Jesus told his twelve disciples that "if anyone would come after me, he must deny himself and take up his cross daily and follow me. For whoever wants to save his life will lose it, but whoever loses his life for me will save it" (Lk 9:23–24). This proclamation coming straight out of Jesus Christ's mouth is the cornerstone to salvation in its entirety. Without comprehending the importance of denying yourself, the essence of walking the Christian walk is incomplete.

This brings us to the subject of temptation. Sinning is a result of temptation. Temptation is that enticing urge to go against what we know is right for the short-term effects gratification brings. There are irrefutably pleasures in the sins we commit, but these pleasures do not justify our actions when we commit sin. Moreover, sin separates us from God. This is why Christians must learn to deny themselves to successfully walk in righteousness—the level of righteousness that God is pleased with. There is a whole host of barriers that keep us from drawing closer to God in our walk with Jesus Christ. Sexual immorality, greed, riches, lying, stealing, and pride are among the wide array of sin. There is a myriad of sins that can alter believers on their path of righteousness. Practicing self-discipline can make us stronger because it will help us build a tolerance for denying ourselves. The pleasures of sin will ultimately only last for a season, which is the reason why suffering affliction will always trump the decision of giving into sin. Jesus told his disciples that they would need to pick up their crosses and follow him in order to save their own lives. To do this means to crucify yourself and the vices that are holding you down from a life of righteousness and God's abundant blessings.

I'd like to tell the story of a wonderful man by the name of Ron. I met Ron because he was dating a friend of mine's grandmother. Ron was a kindhearted man who was like a snow-ball when he would explain himself to you. He would start off small, rolling slowly with not much momentum, until he gathered more and more details that painted his picture more definitively. Once Ron got the momentum from recalling details of a particular matter, he was much like a snowball turned into a large snow boulder rolling downhill. By the time he hit this rate of conveying his story with such detail, everyone within a ten-foot radius was on board for the ride, enthralled with his hand gestures and animated acting. Ron gave me his testimony that was closely linked with the use and abuse of cocaine. Ron told me how for nine years he was completely addicted to cocaine. These nine years passed like a flash to him due to the frequent sedation the drug offered him.

Then on one evening, Ron decided he was going to fight the beast that had imprisoned him for so long. The truth of the matter was that Ron was ready for a change, a change for the better. As Ron used hand motions and attention-demanding gestures, he described to me the very night he decided cocaine was not going to enslave him anymore. He described that night of breakthrough as his typical Friday night at a close friend's house. This friend of Ron's had been throwing a party that involved the usual cocaine and alcohol. Ron remembered feeling a sense of emptiness that night, more so than ever before. He described the feeling he had as one of discontentment.

"Everyone was indulging in business as usual, oblivious to their problems or worries," Ron said to me. "But then, everyone fell asleep, and I myself was all alone with the leftover piles of cocaine and remaining alcohol bottles that had plenty of liquor left in them." Ron, with a serious gaze in his eyes behind his glasses he wore, further explained, "My thoughts began to hone in on truth, wondering just what truth was. I pondered what God had to say about my lifestyle and, to be honest, if God even cared."

By this time my emotions were anxious to hear how Ron chose to handle this event in his life. Ron began again, "I decided to cry out to God for help in finding truth because I did not believe that the lifestyle or the frame of mind I had happened to be in during that time was truth. So when I turned on the television, there was a program on that swayed me to Jesus Christ's salvation. I looked on the table where there was a mound of cocaine and a big bottle of alcohol." At that point Ron asked me, "Do you know how when a bottle goes from being nice and cold to room temperature, how it sweats and looks all seductive?"

"Yes," I replied.

"This is exactly how the full bottle appeared that night to me when I looked at it." Ron went on to tell me that it crossed his mind that this was a choice to either get rid of his headache that he had or to start fresh on a new path that God had laid out for him. Ron knew that if he were to take the drugs and alcohol, it would have been a quick fix to his immediate problem yet an investment, so to speak, in his long-term addiction. Ron said that if he had chosen the easy decision—taking the cocaine and alcohol as opposed to denying himself—the vicious cycle of enslavement would reset, only to be more of a bondage to him. Ron chose to cease his addictions that very night and give his life over to Jesus Christ as his Lord and savior. This, friends, is the type of surrender that all can benefit from. Bondage was not meant for the children of God. When the subject of surrender is discussed in regard to surrendering to Jesus Christ, it is not to force you into an arduous life of dissatisfaction, but rather a life of deliverance unto bigger, better things!

Countless examples in the Bible supply us with occurrences of this taking place. The twelve disciples that accompanied Jesus were challenged to leave their lives to follow along with him in order to achieve greater things, such as preaching the Gospel and obtaining holiness in the sight of the Lord. Peter happened to be fishing one day when Jesus told him that he would make Peter a fisher of men, indicating that God had much greater plans for his life than to simply catch fish. Abraham was challenged to sacrifice his son Isaac because God needed to know that Abraham believed in God enough and trusted in God's will for his life. God did not wind up having Abraham kill his son Isaac on the altar, but he did do something in Abraham's life that was astonishing. Abraham's wife, Sarah, is the oldest recorded woman to give birth to this day! Another amazing blessing God granted Abraham was to inherit a foreign land. Abraham was asked by God to travel to a foreign land that he was completely new to. Just imagine being requested to travel to a foreign country you knew absolutely nothing about and set up camp. For many, this would seem an arbitrary request. For others it may also seem dictatorial. However, Abraham did just as God asked due to a strong value that he held. This value, friends, is called "surrender." Knowing what we know about the Son of God and that God is a God of love, should we really fear surrendering to such a sovereign Lord? I don't think so. Abraham surely did not emotionally agree with what was asked of him. In spite of how he may have felt, his actions revealed the condition of his heart, which is just what God looks at in regard to us as people. In Proverbs 21:2, God speaks to us, saying, "A person may think their own ways are right, but the Lord weighs the heart."

Make sure that the heart is in the right place when making decisions. God smiles when we do this because this is the thing that he looks at when evaluating our motives. Salvation is available to anyone who is courageous enough to accept it. Greatness lies in salvation, and it's waiting on those of us who will only be so wise as to unclench our fists to our own flawed ways of thinking and live for Jesus. If you'd like to accept Jesus into your life today and receive his eternal love and gift of eternal life, then pray these simple words as you read this text aloud: "Lord, I am a sinner; forgive me of my sins and come into my life so that I may live for you. Make me new in your eyes as I surrender my life for your will. Amen."

CHAPTER 2

THE CORRIDOR

NOW THAT YOU HAVE HAD the wonderful opportunity to accept the eternal gift of salvation, we shall talk about the spiritual walk of a believer in Christ. The spiritual walk can be defined as an ongoing battle of your flesh versus your spirit. The flesh has many desires that are healthy, while other fleshly desires aren't so healthy at all when it comes to preserving the holiness of the spirit. Fleshly desires are often impulsive and produce a short-term effect of pleasure. As believers in Christ, we must identify these fleshly desires that are not warranted by God in order to avoid being distanced from God in our spiritual walk of righteousness. This ongoing battle between the flesh and the spirit is precisely the corridor I speak of that lies between greatness and insanity. Because we are only humans made imperfectly, our minds have a tendency to digress, leading eventually to sin. This corridor between God's greatness for your life and your own insanity is crucial to recognize because it is a great adversary to believers in Christ.

While Jesus Christ is rooting for your spirit, meaning pureness in every sense of the word, the other guy, Satan, is salivating at the mouth for you to fall into temptation. In other words, the devil is happy for evil actions to take place because they further separate you from God. God, on the other hand, wants believers to practice becoming more like his Son, Jesus Christ, because it draws us closer to God's greatness for our lives. With God being the Creator and the devil serving as an imitator, which side would you rather draw closer to? God loves and cherishes your life; he wants the very best for you now, in the future, and forever to come. The devil wishes to consume you with empty promises and artificial glitter when what God offers is gold. Think about what glitter is composed of compared to the precious metal of gold. Glitter has no real value to it; no sustaining value anyhow. Glitter is used for decoration and cheap sparkle. Gold is entirely different. Gold retains its value, and its glimmer does not falter. It is much more pure, much more reliable. This is a useful illustration to keep in mind when evaluating the difference in value between following the flesh versus following the Spirit of the Lord.

God is love, and we are instructed to love one another. Loving one another is the underlying purpose God has for all of our lives. We are to love one another as we love ourselves. We are to love our friends, love our families, and yes, even love our enemies. Loving our enemies can be hard at times because people can be cruel and obscene. There are some people that we come across that simply get the best of us. Some people are downright obnoxious beyond logic, making it very easy to want to react in an inappropriate manner.

If you ever need someone to relate to when you feel you are being mistreated, I challenge you to consider Jesus Christ. Jesus

Christ was a perfectly sinless individual that only exuded love to everyone he came into contact with. This did not seem to matter because in the end, the people punished him anyway. There is nothing as unfair to someone as the way the people treated Jesus. He extended love, and the people crucified him. Don't let anyone provoke you to lose a blessing in Christ. Know that God will return any due vengeance on the wicked. Situations such as wrongful accusations, the slandering of your name, and spiteful gestures should only be looked at as opportunities to become more like Christ because he in fact suffered the same oppression from the masses while living on earth. Continue to love, and you shall be rewarded for it with rich blessings. The Bible tells us to not worry about afflictions suffered due to others' actions upon us, for it is God's justice to repay. In 2 Thessalonians, it reads, "God is just: he will pay back trouble to those who trouble you and give relief to you who are troubled, and to us as well. This will happen when the Lord Jesus is revealed from heaven in blazing fire with his powerful angels" (2 Thes 1:6–7). Fret not, because to suffer the same way Christ suffered is a blessing. There is no higher form of understanding outside of experiencing something for yourself.

Throughout the Bible, examples of fierce battles between the flesh and spirit carry on and are quite useful to anyone who evaluates the lessons they entail. Namely, the Israelites were constantly faced with earthly desires as opposed to following the Spirit, or God's will. The Israelites began in complete poverty, as they were under control of the mighty pharaoh in Egypt. God used Moses to deliver the Israelites from slavery out of Egypt, and they escaped by way of the Red Sea when Moses parted the ocean with the power of the Lord. Not only did the Israelites witness this miracle of God but other miracles as well.

God performed other miracles via Moses's staff, such as turn- ing a body of water into blood. He also allowed the Israelites to witness plagues placed upon the Egyptians. Also, the Israelites were left alone for forty days and forty nights when their lead- er, Moses, went up on Mount Sinai to consult with God. When Moses came back down from Mount Sinai after forty days and forty nights, the Israelites had made themselves a golden calf to worship. This may have been senseless enough, but to make matters worse, they failed again when they decided to turn away from God while traveling to the desert. You may ask, How could people be literally escorted through the Red Sea by the hand of God, only to worship a golden calf? The answer to this question is simply the loss of faith. When we lose faith, giving in to the flesh becomes more and more enticing. The attractiveness of fol- lowing the flesh is hard enough to deal with alone, but the loss of faith in God exponentially reduces the believers' chances to win this battle. We must have an unwavering trust in the Lord in order to effectively thwart the temptations we have. How many times are we faced in life with the urge to commit sins that only separate us further from God? You should make the conscious decision to rely on the power of God to foil Satan's plans to de- grade you as a believer.

DRAW CLOSER
This can be executed through prayer and studying the Bible. A powerful verse to be retained from the book of Isaiah is found in chapter 59, which tells us that sin separates us from God. The verse reads, "Surely the arm of the Lord is not too short to save, nor his ear to dull to hear. But your iniquities have separated you from your God; your sins have hidden his face from you, so

that he will not hear you" (Is 59:1–2). The take-home meaning of this is that the iniquities in us distance us from God's greatness for our lives. I personally do not want this for you; it is a great loss to have the Lord Almighty turn away from us. Let me clarify that sin is not going to create an everlasting chasm between the Lord and believers. However, God will distance himself from us if we are continually disobeying his Word. God explains to us in Isaiah that there is no peace for the wicked. Sin and wickedness are a bottomless pit that cannot be satisfied. Sin is truly insatiable. Listen to what the Lord reveals to us in the book of Isaiah. Isaiah 32:16–17 reads, "Justice will dwell in the fertile land. The fruit of righteousness will be peace; the effect of righteousness will be quietness and confidence forever." You too can have this peace and confidence the Lord Almighty speaks of in this text.

The mysteries of the Lord are found in obeying his instruction, instruction from a Father who loves you as a daughter or son of his kingdom! Peace is sought out among the masses; it has been chased after by those that desire the tranquility and satisfaction peace brings. We witness the attempt of finding peace in the multitude of sedatives humanity indulges in on a regular basis. In mentioning sedatives, I speak not only of the actual sedative drugs in the world but also of the avenues that are generally traveled down for some type of relief in a person's life. For some it may be sex. For another group of people it may be drugs. Others may find sedation in the excessive intake of food, also known as gluttony. In the midst of the great search for peace, we find ourselves getting trapped in the ridiculous lottery game of trial and error. The problem with this method is that too many of us get stuck in the vortex of one of those trials by way of addiction. Our mind-set toward addictive substances is similar to our mind-set toward caffeine: we understand that coffee and energy drinks are not permanent cures for exhaustion, but we settle because they give the relief we desire for that particular moment. Isaiah 48:18 reveals the essence of peace to believers in Christ: "If only you had paid attention to my commands, your peace would have been like a river, your righteousness like the waves of the sea. Your descendants would have been like the sand, your children like its numberless grains; their name would never be cut off nor destroyed from before me." According to this verse, abiding by the counsel of the Holy Bible produces a peace within us. God wishes that his children would act according to the commands he has set into place because he is the potter and we are the clay. Isaiah 45:9 reads, "Woe to him who quarrels with his maker, to him who is but a potsherd among the potsherds on the ground. Does the clay say to the potter, 'What are you making?' Does your work say, 'He has no hands'?" Furthermore, Isaiah 64:8 tells us again, "Yet, oh Lord, you are our father. We are the clay, you are the potter; we are all the work of your hands."

A MEDICAL STORY

At 2:30 a.m. the piercing emergency tones sounded off, waking me from a serene slumber. The emergency dispatcher notified my station that there was cardiac arrest call in need of our attention. Quickly stepping into my jumpsuit that had reflectors on it for the sake of nighttime visual clarity, I grabbed my belt, which had a radio clasped onto it, and frantically buckled the belt around my waist. My partner, Brian, and I simultaneously read the call notes, which informed the two of us that CPR was in progress. En route to the call, Brian and I discussed what roles each of us were going to assume once on scene of the call. We agreed that my role would be to place the defibrillation pads on the patient and manage initiating an IV in order to push medications. Brian's role was to manage the patient's airway up to and including a procedure called intubation. We grabbed our emergency airway bag, the cardiac monitor, the suction unit, our medications bag, and the Intraosseous drill kit. We rushed into the patient's house and saw two firefighters performing CPR and an emotional male spouse concerned about his thirty-four-year-old wife that was on the ground lying unconscious. After placing the defibrillation pads and starting an IV, we pushed the initial medication of epinephrine. The spouse was doing everything within his will to hold back his emotional distress as he witnessed us trying to resuscitate his wife. The spouse stated that his wife had overdosed on heroin and that he felt it was a suicide attempt. A drug that emergency medical services directs us to give in our protocol for suspected narcotic overdoses (heroin being a narcotic) is a medication named Narcan. This particular medication binds with cell receptors to reverse the effects of narcotics. Following an administration of Narcan, CPR continued. Our crew gave an extended effort to resuscitate this young woman, but we were unsuccessful in doing so. My partner, Brian, had successfully intubated the patient, high-quality CPR was initiated, and the timing of drugs couldn't have been more punctual. When defibrillating (shocking) a patient, they must have a shockable rhythm on the cardiac monitor, which was never present, so defibrillation did not occur.

Shortly after we stopped our efforts, this young woman was reluctantly pronounced dead. The release of sorrow in her husband's voice was wrenching. Emotional wreckage was at full force as the husband spoke through tears, saying, "She talked a lot about suicide, but I never thought it would actually happen!" The crew and I earnestly attempted to console the husband, who had been overwhelmed by what had just come to pass. These calls are among the worst in this line of work because you never want to see anyone lose their loved one, be it a significant other, family member, or close friend. The distress that consumes the individuals involved is unforgiving and unwavering in the midst of the moment. When all efforts have been exhausted, the only thing left for the person suffering the loss of the loved one is to mourn. Here you have a young woman who reportedly spoke often about suicide and ended up performing just that. In that corridor that lies between greatness and insanity, dark things reside. Cryptic in nature, these dark things exist in all of our minds and can be dangerous if the right solution is not pursued. Jesus Christ is the solution to avoid such dangers of the mind because Jesus Christ supplies us with the irrefutable strength to battle anything we may be facing. The corridor I speak of is not limited to the damage it can bestow upon an individual, and this medical story shows the essence of what could potentially happen in the more severe cases of letting that corridor get the best of you.

When I ponder medical calls such as this one, my heart can't help but hope that the individual at hand was a Christian. My goal is to reach as many as God's will allows me to in order to minister to the souls who need the gift of salvation. Death is the one earthly fate we will all inevitably have to come face-to-face with. My question to the reader is, do you know where you will be going once you die? See, my complete concern for you is that the salvation that is readily available to you be given to you. As I explained in the previous chapter, all you have to do is believe and then ask Jesus Christ into your heart after admitting to him wholeheartedly that you are an imperfect sinner. My intention is not to dangle the thought of death in front of you as an intimidation or scare tactic. Nor do I wish to create an environment in which you suddenly feel rushed or forced into receiving a false hope or gift. This gift of eternal salvation is true, and accepting it is the most important decision you must make in life. The Bible sheds love on those that believe through holy instruction. Jesus tells us that he is the way, the truth, and the light. I have put countless hours into the study of the Bible in order to comprehend the messages God wants us all to retain. Think about your own life and what may be missing from it. Purpose is found in God, and without purpose, life makes no sense at all.

King Solomon wrote about purpose in Ecclesiastes, where the phrase *nothing new under the sun* was coined. Solomon was a man of great wealth, power, and influence. Solomon also was a lover of women, for he had seven hundred wives and three hundred concubines, making a grand total of one thousand lovers! In Ecclesiastes, Solomon writes of his many endeavors in his life that he may have enjoyed but could not find much meaning in when it all came down to it. Solomon, being a king, had access to virtually anything he wanted to toil in, and he did so. I would like to point out the fact that although Solomon had so many wives and concubines, this was not God's will, and Solomon was indeed punished by the Lord. Even though Solomon did not follow all the wisdom that he was endowed with from God, he was spot-on in his conclusion to the purpose of life. Solomon concluded that without God involved in your life, life essentially makes no sense. King Solomon was not a perfect man, but he does happen to be the wisest man in recorded history. The Bible itself says that no other man was wiser, for God had given him the wisdom of the Lord. Ecclesiastes 12:13–14 says, "Now all has been heard; here's the conclusion of the matter: Fear God and keep his commandments, for this is the whole duty of man. For

God will bring every deed into judgment, including every hidden thing, whether it is good or evil." The wisest man in all of history who was granted the Lord's own wisdom wrote this, so we can be confident that as believers, our whole duty on earth is to keep God's commands. We were all created for the purpose of loving one another while keeping all of God's instructions on the tablets of our hearts and minds.

The relationship we must develop with Jesus Christ is what will be judged when God evaluates who shall be worthy enough to enter the gates of heaven. God is going to ask his Son, Jesus, if you knew him or not. Another question God will evaluate among us is the question of whether each of us kept the commandments that God instructed us to hold on to, not only being hearers of the word but doers of the word. Faith without works is not very useful at all. We are told in James 1:22–25, "Do not merely listen to the word, and so deceive yourselves. Do what it says. Anyone who listens to the word but does not do what it says is like a man who looks at his face in the mirror and, after looking at himself, goes away and immediately forgets what he looks like. But the man who looks intently into the perfect law that gives freedom, and continues to do this, not forgetting what he has heard, but doing it—he will be blessed in what he does." Focus your energy on carrying out God's commands.

This is the true challenge for your life because the simple pleasures have such eye-catching effects. Don't be fooled by the facades sin constructs; the result of sin is the distancing from God. Building a relationship is meant to be a close, intimate endeavor with the Lord, not an estranged, distanced experience. When we keep the commands of the perfect law God has created, our greatness is realized. Sinning creates complacency and stagnancy and generally stunts our growth in the Lord. At this time we will review some of the ways that you can effectively thwart the impending doom that the corridor can inject you with. As with any battle, efficient preplanning and strategy must be applied for us to stand a chance. Spiritual warfare is no different. In fact, spiritual warfare can be dealt with if we just properly prepare for the battle. There are six effective ways to mitigate the state of complacency the corridor can trap you in. These six techniques are prayer, practicing denial, isolation, goals, the development of hobbies, and reading the Word.

PRAYER

Prayer can be greatly utilized for strengthening believers. A good practice to start the day when you wake up is to set aside a few minutes to have a talk with God. The Lord yearns to hear what is on our hearts and in our minds. Just as someone may phone a friend to get something off his or her chest, this is the same manner in which believers must become comfortable in communicating with God. Communication, as it is in any relationship, is critical in maintaining a bond. The length and strength of any relationship is often measured by how well the two involved persons communicate. Prayer is your direct line to God himself. My father would joke with me at times when he used to ask me to say the prayer for the family at the dinner table. Before I would begin praying, he sometimes would rib me by abruptly saying, "Are you sure your prayers can get through the ceiling?" It was all in good fun, but there is much validity to be considered in the playful joking my dad did at the dinner table. Because sin separates us from God, this factor in our praying can play a tremendous role in effective prayer.

An area of prayer that deserves maximum attention is our intentions in doing so. God does not willfully honor hearts that have ulterior motives. Proverbs 21:2 explains, "A person may think their own ways are right, but the Lord weighs the heart." The ulterior motives that I speak of are precisely the motives that are in contrast with God's will. Another thing believers must be on watch for is their personal righteousness. A person cannot be living in the thick of all sin and then become disoriented and disarrayed with the fact that they feel as though God is ignoring them. God answers prayers, but God is on his own time, not ours. It would be so convenient if God were to answer all of our prayers as soon as we send them up to him. Prayer doesn't work this way. God is interested in what we're made of, meaning how faithful we will remain, even when he is seemingly absent from our lives. God may sometimes respond to prayer more expediently than other times, but don't get discouraged if his will for you is to wait longer than you are comfortable.

Saul of Kish is an excellent example of when waiting on a response segued into a very unwise decision. Saul, from the tribe of Benjamin, was the son of Kish and the first king of Israel. The Bible explains in 1 Samuel that the Philistines were out to destroy Saul. Unfortunately Saul had turned his ways away from the ways of the Lord; therefore the Lord had turned away from Saul. At this particular time, King Saul was under a massive amount of stress, as you could imagine. King Saul literally had a bounty on his head from the Philistines. The judge Samuel was no longer living, and King Saul had been dependent upon Samuel when it came to consulting with the Lord. King Saul consistently prayed about direction because he was looking for a way to evade the Philistine attack. Instead of being patient and waiting on the Lord, he grew so impatient that he looked to other entities. He ended up consulting a medium out of fear for his life to tell him what would happen to him. Now let's take the time to think about ourselves and how we may have reacted negatively in the past when we're anxious to hear from the Lord. King Saul was in a valley of decision to remain faithful, as his life was allegedly nearing destruction due to the Philistines. This expiration of trust in God that Saul exemplified was not pleasing to the Lord whatsoever. Saul summoned Samuel via a medium because while on earth Samuel had proved to be a reliable communicator with God. The oracle that Samuel revealed to King Saul was that Saul was going to die by the hands of the Philistines along with his three sons. This biblical story is not to inflict fear upon the reader, but rather to serve as a learning experience to steer clear of hiccups such as the mistake King Saul made. We can clearly see that the Lord Almighty was in total disapproval of King Saul's turning to a medium for advice. Since the subject of witchcraft is now fresh in the mind, allow me to attest from personal experience that witchcraft is indeed real and very much alive.

My Meeting with the Tarot Card Reader

When I was twenty-one years old, my girlfriend and I had time to burn. It was summertime, and the only thing we had on our minds was adventure. This was during a period of time in my life where the desire for thrills exceeded my desire for wisdom. I will be the first one to tell you that this was an immature mistake that could and should have been avoided. My curiosity was pulsating like a fully involved structure fire, and my girlfriend had no inhibitions about checking something mysterious out either.

The plan was to visit a psychic because we both had always wondered if the innumerable psychic shops you see on the side of the road were real or fake. My feelings were that even if no truth was to be found in the fortunetelling, the entertainment itself would be comical. We arrived at the psychic's shop and sat in the car for a second collecting our thoughts. After knocking on the door, a hobbit-like woman opened the door slowly and signaled us both to enter. I introduced myself and my girlfriend, and the short, stocky woman returned our greeting with a big smile that spanned across her face from ear to ear. What I saw next was disturbing to say the least. The most grotesque set of teeth and gums were exposed when she smiled. The woman's front four teeth in the center, both bottom and top, were the largest, thickest teeth I have ever seen in my life! It was peculiar, for her center four teeth on both bottom and top looked as if they were molars. The older lady wasted no time in telling my girlfriend and me that she only does private one-on-one sessions. My suspicion was now at a climax due to her ghoul-like appearance coupled with her expressed desire to evaluate us in private. We went ahead and followed through with the plan to experience this mysterious session. My girlfriend waited in the other room while I was undergoing a tarot card reading session in a back room that had only a table and chairs in it. The short, rugged woman began her routine and told me many things that were what I will refer to as "relatively intangible." She threw out a whole host of immeasurable, broad statements that did set off events in my life that immediately came into my thoughts. In my mind I had made a rule to not give in to anything she said, maintaining a neutral face. The last thing I wanted was to give the woman a lead to run with and feed off of. Finally it came: a tarot card reading that could be tested. The mysterious woman professed to me that my financial status was going to change considerably in six weeks. This particular day was a Monday. I locked that into my memory bank like someone could remember his or her favorite dessert. When I made it home, I marked my calendar and marked the subsequent six Mondays that followed. Interestingly enough, I received a phone call that sixth Monday from the local fire department. My goal had been to get recruited with my hometown fire department, and in the meantime I was working part-time with a private ambulance company. So sure enough, the tarot card reader nailed it on the head; she predicted a financial change of income six weeks from our session. In exactly six Mondays from the Monday my girlfriend and I visited her, my monetary earning power shifted into a higher gear.

Don't be misled or fooled by thinking that witchcraft is something to toy with or an entertaining outing like I did. God does not approve of this behavior at all. God Almighty is the one sovereign God and the only sovereign God. When people get misdirected in the paths of experimentation, it opens up the spiritual gates to more witchcraft or other venues that separate us from God.

The role of the believer is to pray and seek knowledge for God's will. You'd be surprised that some individuals spend great deals of money on consistently visiting mediums. The astonishment of seeking what will happen next in their lives gets them hooked like a hungry fish on a baited hook. Witchcraft is very real, but its power source is not from the Lord. Give caution to those you may hear indulging in such activities because it is a complete misdirection. God's will is more important than what a medium or psychic can tell you about yourself or family. Christians' line of communication is prayer and repetitious study of the Holy Word.

PRACTICING DENIAL

The next line of defense you should develop in battling the flesh versus the spirit is the discipline of denying yourself. Jesus said to his disciples that if anyone is to follow him, that person must be willing to take up his or her cross (deny him or herself) in order to be successful in doing so (Lk 9:23). Are you going to kick back, fold your hands, and let the spiritual war defeat you? In being a generally easygoing person in most things, I can personally tell you that the battle for your mind is not one you can contest with by having a passive approach to it. Let the reader understand that this war for your spirit has to be aggressively dealt with. Personally, I'm a competitive individual with a competitive frame of mind. Every now and then when I'm in the heat of a battle on the basketball court or the soccer field, the amount of trash talk I dish out to my opponents is an attempt to derail their focus. One of my favorite things to say is, "You can't ignore me; you can't just make me disappear; the only thing you can do is *deal* with me!" So now I will tell you it's the same about the heated battle for your spirit and mind: "You can't ignore it! You can't make it disappear! All you can do is *deal* with it!"

In the area of denying the self, practice is your most prized ally to building tolerance to self-denial. Denying yourself is the very skill that keeps you from committing crimes, jumping off of a cliff, or shouting obscenities in public. It's intriguing the way one thing is easier to deny than another. These different impulses and temptations have to do with how we are genetically made coupled with the way we think. Denying yourself is not just a matter of proclaiming that you're not going to do something ever again. Accountability has to be the primary factor in this technique of dealing effectively with the spiritual battle for your mind. A great way to create accountability is to make your decision known. Make your decision to deny yourself (in whichever way it may be) openly in front of someone by simply telling them. Openly confess your problem or issue to other believers so that they can pray for you. Now there will be a core group of individuals rooting for you, and it will not be as easy to let them down as opposed to merely letting yourself down. Practice does not make you perfect, but it sure does make you better. Consistently develop the mind-set to deny what may be a negative thing in your life by actively practicing abstinence from it. Keep in mind that God can see what man cannot see. God is watching our efforts—even the ones that occur when we are alone.

ISOLATION

The third way of helping fight the war for your mind is isolation. This method can be pretty hardcore. In this method, you must isolate yourself from that which is ailing your spiritual connection with God. In the Bible, King Nebuchadnezzar unfortunately was isolated for a period of time, but not of his own accord. The pressing issue King Nebuchadnezzar dealt with was pride. This falls under one of the three categories that all sin falls under. The three categories that all sins irrevocably fall under are the pride of life, the lust of the flesh, and the lust of the eyes. King Nebuchadnezzar had become so arrogant that he ordered his men to create an image of gold that stood ninety feet tall and nine feet wide. His enlightening story is found in the book of Daniel. King Nebuchadnezzar experienced dreams that were interpreted by Daniel. The final dream Daniel interpreted for King Nebuchadnezzar was his punishment, the discipline that God was going to carry out. God drove the king out into the wilderness like a beast of the field, causing him to lose his sanity. Daniel 4:33 says, "Immediately what had been said about Nebuchadnezzar was fulfilled. He was driven away from people and ate grass like cattle. His body was drenched with the dew of heaven until his hair grew like the feathers of an eagle and his nails like the claws of a bird." Pride is a vice for many that will not be honored by the Lord. Pride prohibits followers of God from spiritual maturity by impeding upon God's will for our lives. God despises haughty eyes and a proud walk. Arrogance consumes individuals by making them think the work of their hands was just that, a work of only their own hands, when in reality it was a blessing from God. King Nebuchadnezzar was isolated so that his pride could not stand in his own way. God's way of humbling him was extreme, yes, but the extent of pride King Nebuchadnezzar had held was phenomenal just the same.

Returning to God's ways is what all must do when we fall to sin. God understands our imperfections, so we can be sure that his grace will be our *saving* grace. Beware of pride, for it is meaningless. Your pride, my pride, or anyone's pride is not conducive to carrying out God's will. Knowing that God will allow you to return to him is not any reason at all to have to bear the painful and not to mention avoidable discipline God will incur upon our lives to get us back on track for his divine purposes. God did what he always does to those he loves, as we read in the Daniel 4:34: "At the end of time, I, Nebuchadnezzar, raised my eyes toward heaven, and my sanity was restored. Then I praised the most high; I honored and glorified him who lives forever." He continues giving God praise and acknowledges that the Lord is all-powerful, doing what he pleases in all accounts of everything.

One thing that makes me smile when I think about the Lord is how faithful he is to those who believe. King Nebuchadnezzar is actually increased in greatness after his discipline: "At the same time that my sanity was restored, my honor and splendor were returned to me for the glory of my kingdom. My advisors and nobles sought me out, and I was restored to my throne and became even greater than before. Now I, Nebuchadnezzar, praise and exalt and glorify the King of heaven, because everything he does is right in all his ways are just. And those who walk in pride he is able to humble" (Dn 4:36–37). We are painted a vivid picture of what God had planned for the prideful Nebuchadnezzar. His mind had turned to self-glorification rather than the purposes God wanted, and therefore God intervened. God will always intervene on behalf of those that he loves. He is a father to us. Isn't it profoundly interesting that God disciplined the king yet showed him grace by adding more to him than before, just as the Lord added more to Job after he suffered? King Nebuchadnezzar had become stagnant in that corridor that lies between greatness and insanity with his elevated pride. The monumental expression with both Job and Nebuchadnezzar's period of suffering was the afterward exaltation of God. In both stories, thanks and gratification toward the Lord was on the forefronts of their hearts. Isolation, as we can learn from the book of Daniel, can be very effective in helping us deny ourselves.

CREATING GOALS

I'd like to now discuss the importance of building goals in relation to abstaining from the fleshly desires of the heart. A critical way of reducing the vulnerability that chasing after the flesh can foster is the creation of meaningful goals. Do not confuse a dream with a goal. The difference is this: dreams have no deadline or expiration date, but goals do. This goes back to the accountability principle discussed. It's great to set high standards for yourself and put forth the effort toward the standards, but what is going to push you to achieving these standards? The answer is deadlines. Furthermore, the creation of meaningful goals in your life puts you in a position to follow a predetermined regimen, making any deviation from the regimen a time-sensitive occurrence that may prohibit your goals from being achieved! As believers, we should view goal setting as a cornerstone for achieving God's greatness because it gives a set of directions to follow for ourselves. If you find that your fleshly desires are keeping you from staying close to God, a bigger goal is a healthy thing to acquire. Establishing a goal that counteracts your fleshly desires is the type of goal all should pursue. Invent a goal great enough that makes what you may be battling a nuisance to your righteous desires. The great prophet Isaiah was going through a tough time in his life according to the Bible in Isaiah chapter 49. Isaiah told God that he had labored in vain! Imagine feeling as though all your hard work had no meaning behind it; how miserable of an endeavor would that be? God's answer to Isaiah was this: get a *larger* goal. Expand your vision a bit broader, servant. "It is too small a thing for you to be my servant to restore the tribes of Jacob and bring back those of Israel I have kept. I will also make you a light for the Gentiles, that you may bring my salvation to the ends of the earth" (Is 49:6). Too often the goal at hand is not large enough; this is the result of confining God's power to a box. With God on our side, there is no box. There is no boundary as to what we can achieve according to his will. Get out of the constrictions of limiting the dreams you have to something small. God is great; therefore our goals should reflect the greatness of our God. After all, he is the Alpha and the Omega, the Creator of all things. Limiting your goals and dreams is the equivalent to putting a leash on yourself. When you do this, you are settling for less before even going for the prize. Here is what Ephesians reveals to believers about God. In his concluding prayer, the apostle Paul writes, "Now to him who is able to do immeasurably more than all we ask or imagine, according to his power that is at work within us, to him be glory in the church and in Christ Jesus throughout all generations, forever and ever! Amen" (Eph 3:20–21). The Lord's power is unlimited. As children of the Lord, our actions and goals should reflect this truth with the size of our ambition. Life will produce burdens that are hefty in nature, but we must not fold.

One thing my father taught me in one of his clever phrases was, "You have to know when to hold and know when to fold." The relevance of this witty line is choosing your battles with wisdom, but what I'd like to touch on more acutely is forgetting the burdens that are better left forgotten. Pressing onward is the art of creating new success. Yes, it is true, the burdens that rest on our shoulders are often the results of decisions we personally made, but no one can change the past. You do have control in the future decisions you make, however, so learning lessons can be considered a spiritual responsibility because God longs for his children to establish larger, more robust goals. Listen to what the apostle Paul says about the subject of goals in his letter to the Philippians: "Brothers, I do not consider myself yet to have taken hold of it. But one thing I do: forgetting what is behind and straining toward what is ahead, I press on toward the *goal* to win the prize for which God has called me heavenward in Christ Jesus" (Phil 3:13–15). Traveling in the direction of our goals is in opposition to idleness. Idleness is often a person's Achilles' heel. Too much free time without having anything to occupy the mind allows useless thoughts to infest the desires of men.

DEVELOPMENT OF HOBBIES

Method number five for battling the flesh is to keep busy with a plethora of activities. The idea is to keep yourself on the move so that the deviation from spiritual holiness is not so easily done. For instance, establishing and maintaining hobbies is an excellent way to exercise the mind and body in a healthy way. I grew up playing soccer. My church has been blessed to have a sports ministry where every Sunday, the soccer players of the church get together at a local sports complex and play pickup soccer. During halftime, a message from the Bible is shared, serving as a time of fellowship. We actually had a gentleman speak one Sunday who had been on the national team for the country of Brazil. His testimony alluded to the passing away of earthly things. He told us of how he had lived the fast life when playing on the Brazil team back in 1989. His message was that during that time, it was all about immediate gratification for him. He stated that he replayed this cycle over and over again until one day he was overwhelmed with the feeling of a void in his life. He stated that he fortunately heard about Jesus and was moved to ask him into his heart. He concluded with saying that he had scored many exciting goals in the professional league while playing, but the most important goal he ever scored was when he gave his life to Christ.

This older gentleman spoke from experience when he warned that everything earthly passes away. Getting involved in church small groups, ministry teams, mission teams, and service positions gives glory to God while helping us avoid idle hands. The mind must be constantly injected with holiness and the like to guard against the destructive plans Satan's will induces. My church even has a traffic team ministry that allows volunteers to direct traffic for services due to the volume of visitors. Practice being proactive in the Lord and in life: this is the nature of accomplishment. Proactivity allows you to be more successful in what you do because reactivity is merely the response to an outside suggestion or idea. Think about it; if an individual were to carry out his or her life with a reactive approach, the results of that person's life would only be the ricochet of what was forced upon him or her through circumstances. More importantly, the circumstances dealt to the individual would have been the circumstances someone else imposed! As children of God, this is not the approach God wants us to take. We are to be creatures of direction, pressing toward God's will for our lives, which is to love and serve others.

READING THE BIBLE

The sixth and final thing I'd like to discuss in regard to battling the corridor that lies between greatness and insanity is the discipline of reading the Bible. In the book of Joshua, the Bible tells us that Moses has died, making Joshua Moses's successor to lead the Israelites. God told Joshua, "Do not let this book of the law depart from your mouth; meditate on it day and night, so that you may be careful to do everything written in it. Then you will be prosperous and successful. Have I not commanded you? Be strong and courageous. Do not be terrified; do not be discouraged for the Lord your God will be with you wherever you go" (Jo 1:8–9). This instruction given to Joshua from God is imperative to inscribe on to our own lives, meaning all believers. Reading the Word of God is reading the handbook or manual on how believers are to live their lives. Any time you buy a new piece of furniture that requires assembly, it is often accompanied by a manual. Any time a consumer buys a product, whether it be a musical device, mechanical device, or even a toy, instructions are given by the manufacturer on the way it is to be utilized. God is the manufacturer, and the Bible is the manual telling us how to live, why we were created, and who we are created for. Neglecting to read the Bible is like neglecting reading the instructions on how to use something. Only the manufacturer can tell you precisely what it was made for and why. Meditating daily on the Word of God refreshes our minds and shields us from the enemies of defeat, confusion, frustration, ignorance, and complacency.

A vastly important thing we gain from reading the Bible is the knowledge of our identity as believers. People have a tendency of somehow losing their way in this challenge called life, but we have been provided a reminder for this very hiccup when it indeed occurs. Biblical instruction is what all may turn to in the event of becoming disarrayed or perplexed about our purpose. The feeling of being lost is one of misery. I pray that you heed this sacred advice to replenish your soul with the mighty Word of God, for I was once lost with much sorrow and agony, on the cusp of insanity.

A Medical Story

The emergency bells rang loud in the station at approximately 6:30 a.m. We had received a call that advised the patient was undergoing diabetic issues, namely hypoglycemia, which is the medical term for low blood sugar. My partner and I scurried out to the ambulance unit with our portable radios in hand. The dispatch notes advised that a male patient, age fifty-five, was not alert due to diabetic complications. On the way to the call, my partner and I discussed what approach to take, as we always do. Upon arriving on scene, we hopped out of the ambulance and pulled our stretcher out of the back doors along with all of our medical bags. We walked inside the house all the way to the back room, where we found a male patient lying unconscious on his back. I immediately checked his blood glucose and began to administer the necessary medication.

After about two minutes of pushing the drug, the patient started to slowly wake up, regaining his coherence. The first thing we asked the patient was, "Are you with us?" In a loud shout, the patient answered, "Yes, I'm with you; yes, I'm with you." We then asked him if he knew what his name was. The patient wasted no time at all in yelling, "I'm Bobby, that's who I am!" In this particular call, he was unable to identify himself when he was not alert. But after being given what he needed to sustain life, he recalled his identity. In the same way, we as believers in Christ must not slip into the pitfall of becoming unconscious to the Word of God in our lives. When we begin thinking that God's Holy Word can be neglected, we then are made into fools. The corridor that lies between God's greatness and our insanity starts to draw in close for our destruction.

IDENTITY

Peter tells us our identity, and we must praise the Lord for having Peter leave his letter for all to examine. Peter so eloquently writes in his letter to believers, "They stumble because they disobey the message—which is also what they were destined for. But you are a chosen people, a royal priesthood, a holy nation, a people belonging to God, that you may declare the praises of him who called you out of darkness into his wonderful light. Once you were a people, but now you are the people of God; once you had not received mercy, but now you have received mercy. Dear friends,

I urge you, as aliens and strangers in the world, to abstain from sinful desires, which war against your soul" (1 Pt 2:9–11). From this verse, there are five things to be dissected and discerned for revealing your identity in life: 1) We are a chosen people. God selected us for greatness as long as we would accept the offer to serve him and believe in him. 2) We are a priesthood—to share the Gospel is a blessing and privilege. 3) We are a holy nation—upon repentance of sin, we were endowed with holiness; namely, the Holy Spirit. 4) We are people of God—we are all God's children, yet we must ask for his Son to enter into our hearts. 5) We have received mercy—mercy was received in order that we could be cleansed of our sins. The song in our hearts should be one of thanks for being the people of such a merciful God.

If you're wondering now what action to implement, refer to 1 Peter, which reveals to us that "each one should use whatever gift he has received to serve others, faithfully administering God's grace in its various forms" (1 Pt 4:10). Some are gifted in writing, others in the areas of singing, sports, teaching, or speaking. Engage your God-given gifts to reach the masses with the story of Jesus. Everyone must be given the chance to receive God's undying love. It is the believer's duty to not be selfish in having this gift but rather proactive in spreading the eternal gift that is available to all.

Do Not Be Discouraged

Do not be discouraged in the battle against sin; even the greatest Christians of all are troubled with the challenges sin presents them. Listen to what Paul says: "So I find this law at work: when I want to do good, evil is right there with me. For in my inner being I delight in God's law; but I see another law at work in the members of my body, waging war against the law of my mind and making me a prisoner of the law of sin at work within my members. What a wretched man I am! Who will rescue me from this body of death? Thanks be to God through Jesus Christ our Lord!" (Rm 7:21–25). Every single person feuds with the temptations of the flesh. The ways of the Spirit are what we must fixate our eyes on. The Bible advises that the ways of the Spirit are in opposition to the flesh. In Galatians, Paul writes, "For the flesh desires what is contrary to the spirit, and the spirit what is contrary to the flesh. They are in conflict with each other, so that you are not to do whatever you want" (Gal 5:17). I encourage you with great urgency to decide in your heart to be a steward of the Spirit's ways because this is God's will for your life. We were not brought here to be impulsive creatures reacting off of feelings. The problem with feelings is that they are not always in stride with what the Spirit desires. For those of you who have subscribed to the popular phrase *follow your heart* or *listen to your heart*, it may burst your bubble to find that this is an inaccurate piece of advice. According to Jeremiah, "The heart is deceitful above all things and beyond cure. Who can understand it?" (Jer 17:9). We'd like to believe that our hearts are always in our best interests when we utilize the heart to make a tough decision. It sounds so appealing to the mind to simply listen to our hearts, and that will shed light on the correct choices in life. This school of thought is false. Referring to scripture in order to unveil God's will is the correct way of making sound decisions. Don't bear all of the weight on your own shoulders; see what God has to say about your dilemmas. The last thing God wants us to do is to exclude his direction from the decisions we make as his children. Just as a father or mother would like to know about his or her young children's decisions and how they can help, so God is concerned for his anointed children. I urge you to become a firmly planted warrior for the ways of the Spirit because doing so leads to peace. The ways of the Spirit foster happiness and contentment.

Meaningless

The ways of the flesh harbor bondage and meaningless repetition. The bondage is never revealed prior to making the choice to live by the fleshly desires, but you'd better believe that the jail cell will undoubtedly encapsulate you after you have committed the crime, so to speak. Humans are creatures of habit. Self-induced habits have the ability to enslave, which makes our decisions all the more unforgiving when making the wrong decision. The nature that habitual sin reflects in our hearts and in our minds is the corridor that lies between greatness and insanity. Choosing the way of the Spirit is to choose greatness for your life. Choosing to enroll in the institution of following the flesh is the way to insanity. Sin is insatiable, as well as the desires of the heart; beware of falling victim to the lies and bondage of the way of the flesh.

Witness the words of a man who cannot quite gain control of himself—this example is the optimal model for what that corridor sounds like: "I know that nothing good lives in me, that is, in my sinful nature. For I have the desire to do what is good, but I cannot carry it out. For what I do is not the good I want to do; no, the evil I do not want to do—this I keep on doing. If I do what I do not want to do, it is no longer I who do it, but it is sin living in me that does it" (Rm 7:18–20). My hope is that you have an open heart to receive the genuine warning of mistaking bondage for pleasure. When you are confused, the Bible is all you need in order to spell out the right way for you. Let us pray.

"Dear Heavenly Father, we come to you in the name of your Son, Jesus Christ, asking that you would bless us with a spirit of discernment. The spiritual warfare is a long-lasting, persistent battle, and we want to be warriors for the Spirit. Give us the tenacity needed to effectively discern good from evil and right from wrong. Bondage is not what your will has planned for us according to your mighty written Word, and we believe that you shall rescue us from this possible bondage. Cover us in your Spirit, Lord. Guide us through our obstacles, for they are so many. At times we will become weary, Lord, but help us to give thanks even in the times of struggle and distress. We thank you for everything you have done in our lives and for allowing each of us to serve you. It is an honor and a holy privilege to be your child, Lord. Allow us to do what is right in all circumstances, not leaning on our own intellect but rather on the written Word you have left for us to examine. We believe in you, we love you, and we look to you to guide each and every one of our steps in life. Amen."

CHAPTER 3
FAITH FOREVER

A MEDICAL STORY

IN THE EARLY-MORNING HOURS OF February 18, 2015, God allowed a special event to occur in my life. He chose a unique time to lay this blessing in my life due to it being in the still of the night at about 3:00 a.m. on a Wednesday. I remember being in a deep dream state on this night, tucked under my covers to shield the cold atmosphere from stealing my warmth. This was the latter portion of my twenty-four hour shift; only about four hours remained until 7:00 a.m. would arrive along with the oncoming crew to change shifts. Just as I repositioned my body in an attempt to maintain a state of comfortable bliss in my station bed, emergency bells rang with piercing intensity that lifted my closed eyelids with brute force. My nighttime suit was positioned to step into along with my steel-toed boots. I try my best to never sleep with my uniform on because of the numerous contaminated environments the calls I respond to are found in. Going to sleep in a pool of bacteria is not the ideal sleeping arrangement for my psyche.

Expeditiously, I slung my radio belt and radio around my waist. My partner and I fled through the station's sliding doors to the ambulance. Upon reading the call notes, my partner, Brian, and I took a brief pause, looking at each other with lumps in our throats. The challenge was as clear as day on the mobile unit computer screen. At 3:00 a.m. on this Wednesday morning, we had been faced with a call to perform an assisted delivery for a twenty-four-year-old female who spoke Spanish. Neither Brian nor I spoke Spanish, so this only added to the size of the lumps in our throats as we proceeded onward toward the call location. Brian and I had a few words with one another as I routed him to the exact road this call was located at. Once out of the ambulance, we sprang to grab our medical bags, heading with intention to the front entrance of the duplex. As we entered the structure, we heard the cries of both a newborn baby and the mother. They were coming from the living room, where the mother was lying down on the couch. Just below her lay a newborn baby on a small bit of towel with the umbilical cord still attached. We laid down our medical bags and frantically put on protective equipment to properly manage the call. My partner then held the umbilical cord as I took a scalpel and cut it, making certain that I would not cut the baby on accident. We warmed and dried the baby, covering his head to keep it warm. The covering of a newborn's head is very important because the head is where newborns can lose a lot of heat, which is dangerous. I handed the newborn to the father to hold, and the father asked, "Is there another one?" As he held up the number two with his fingers, my partner and I suddenly understood there might be twins. Brian went out to retrieve the stretcher. We placed the newborn in the mother's arms once we moved her onto the stretcher for transport to the hospital. We carefully moved across the unleveled yard once getting down the four steps, eager to get this young mother and her child out of the rain into the nearest hospital before the second baby arrived! I reluctantly stepped up into the driver's seat, leaving Brian in the back of the ambulance all alone. Someone had to do the driving, so my focus immediately turned to expedient yet smooth driving. I was careful to make every turn with caution. The back of an ambulance, as you have probably seen, is a big box. The movement in the front of an ambulance (the driver and passenger area) is multiplied by about ten when it comes to the patient compartment (the big box where patient care takes place).

As we pulled into the entrance of the hospital, Brian yelled, "Lorenzo, pull over now! Run into the ER, and grab whoever you can to assist us! She's crowning!" Crowning is when the baby's head can be seen. I returned with a small intervention team of registered nurses and paramedics within about ten seconds. We all facilitated the amazing process of this young woman's second child's birth, which was about twelve minutes after the first newborn. There was a vast amount of blood, creating a lingering scent that left me nauseous. Many paramedics will tell you that they can handle blood and gore but not vomit and mucus. For me, my Achilles' heel is the scent of blood. Fortunately, my threshold for nausea was high enough to keep the contents of my stomach intact.

We transferred the three patients to nurses in the labor and delivery department in the hospital while simultaneously giving our report. Brian looked at me with a look of despair on his face and turned to me, asking, "What on earth was that?" Brian was referring to the herpes around the mother's mouth along with the realization that the mother was completely high on drugs. This information was relayed to Brian and me via one of the nurses who pulled up this young woman's medical history with the hospital that she had accumulated due to being a past patient. They told us that the twenty-four-year-old mother had a history of herpes, cocaine abuse, and prostitution. The twins were not even due until mid-April, and it was only February 18. One nurse even shook her head in dismay once we were in a secluded hallway, saying, "I absolutely hate women that squander their God-given gift of childbirth! My sister can't even have kids! She's often depressed about that as well as me because it's such a misfortune. Meanwhile, you have women like this who could care less about even taking care of their blessing!" I empathized with the nurse, attempting to console her dismay. There had been both greatness and insanity on this day: the greatness being the birth of two new beings; the insanity being the neglected responsibilities of a mother who had been blessed with a healthy enough body to conceive not only one child, but twins.

The newborn twins' future well-being was certainly questionable. When checking back with the labor and delivery department two weeks later, the nurse stated that one of the twins was not doing so well. Be attentive to your blessings. I encourage you to count them as trophies from God. God's blessings are gifts meant to be treated as such, not squandered away like trash. The pleasure was mine in partaking in such an event, although it had not been the ideal scenario due to the mother's condition. God allotted me the experience of my first emergency delivery in the prehospital setting. This particular type of call is special for a paramedic because it is rare that the timing lines up just right in order to be there for the actual delivery. It's all about being in the right place at the right time. God showed us the beautiful work of childbirth as well as the myriad of other blessings he bestows upon our lives. Our job is to be faithful when receiving blessings, for this medical call itself illustrates the truth that not all are blessed with fruitfulness in the same areas of life. Though this truth hurts, the test is to remain faithful in the sight of the Lord because his hand is at work at all times.

DO NOT BE DISHEARTENED, FRIENDS

Do not be afraid or disheartened by the seemingly imbalanced continuum that may upset you. God is the fulcrum when it comes to balance. Faith will see you through any hardship. We all see things that infuriate our minds, leaving thoughts of hopelessness or wrath. God is searching the hearts of believers in these murkiest of times to weigh them. God is interested in your heart in the times that it is not so easy to be thankful. God celebrates the content heart that remains this way under the pressure of trials and tribulations. Do not be surprised when these particular times visit you. Look at tribulations as opportunities to prove your faithfulness in hopes that blessings are on the way. Job says, "Naked I came from my mother's womb, and naked I will depart. The Lord gave and the Lord has taken away; may the name of the Lord be praised" (Jb 1:21). Understanding that God is in control of all things is the assurance believers have when implementing faith. Faith is the gateway to greatness; we see this in the Bible. The beauty of the Bible is that it adds to our contentment in living a faithful life.

Take a stroll with me as I awaken the accounts made available to us through the Holy Bible. These biblical accounts were meant for the strengthening of those who are lacking faith. You can lead a horse to the water, but you can't make it drink. In other words, I will lead you to the truth about faith, but it is up to you to decide to implement this powerful faith in your everyday living. On the other side of this powerful faith is a multitude of blessings God has in store for your life! God rewards the faithful. The book of Hebrews is a monumental book in regard to faith. Hebrews 11:1 reads, "Now faith is confidence in what we hope for, an assurance about what we do not see." The next verse from Hebrews should be written down or underlined in your Bible so that it shall never be forgotten. Hebrews 11:2 reads, "And without faith it is *impossible* to please God, because anyone who comes to him must believe that he exists and that he rewards those who earnestly seek him" (emphasis mine). The key word in this scripture is *impossible*. The Bible stresses to us that pleasing God simply cannot be done in the absence of faith. How important must it be for us to have faith, then, if we desire to please God? Understand that our main purpose for living is for God's glory. Pleasing God is a part of the total picture of our meaning for existence. You weren't created to please yourself for your own benefit while down on earth. No, the meaning for your existence is to keep God's commands, as we learned from Ecclesiastes 12:13–14. The precursor or prerequisite to pleasing God is applying faith. Faith is the single most important value in a believer's life. Fruitfulness stems from faith like branches coming from a tree.

> By faith Abel offered God a better sacrifice than Cain did. By faith Enoch was taken from his life, so that he did not experience death; he could not be found because God had taken him away. For before he was taken away, he was commended as one who pleases God. By faith Noah, when warned about the flood which was not yet seen built the ark. By faith Abraham went to a foreign land that he would later receive as his inheritance. By faith Abraham who was past age and Sarah who was

barren was enabled to become a father because he considered him faithful who had made the promise. By faith, Abraham reasoned that God could raise the dead, and figuratively speaking, he did receive Isaac back from the dead. (Heb 11:4–5, 7–8, 11–19)

The list goes on of faithful warriors.

By faith, Isaac blessed Jacob and Esau in regard to their future. By faith Moses when he had grown up, refused to be known as the son of Pharaoh's daughter. He chose to be mistreated along with the people of God rather than to enjoy the pleasures of sin for a short time. He regarded disgrace for the sake of Christ as a greater value than the treasures of Egypt, because he was looking ahead to his reward. By faith the walls of Jericho fell, after the people had marched around them for seven days. By faith the prostitute Rahab, because she welcomed the spies, was not killed with those who were disobedient. (Heb 11:20, 23–26, 30–31)

It was also by faith that Esther had consulted with the king, even though it may have been at the cost of her life. This was a very courageous move to make in an effort to help her people. The book of Esther reveals, "All the kings officials and the people of the royal provinces know that for any man or woman who approaches the king in the inner court without being summoned the king has but one law: that he be put to death" (Est 4:11). The story of Esther's life in the Bible is a grand illustration of God being in complete control. Esther was unaware that she would become queen. As noted above, she even risked her own life to help her people, and God blessed her. Even when the evil Haman plotted to kill the Jews and Mordecai, Haman ended up being the one who was hanged. Haman's plan due to evil hatred was to have Mordecai hanged, but since God's divine plan was different, the plan backfired on Haman. God hears all and sees all. We must trust in his divine will. When we trust in God's control over all matters, worry is not a dilemma for us. Living a life of worry is not God's plan for us. Believers shall rebuke anxiousness and worry because it is not God's will. Look to the book of Philippians in reference to the worries of life. Recognize them, but put worry and anxiousness in their place where they belong. Worry has no place in the life of a believer. "Do not be anxious about anything, but in every situation, by prayer and petition, with thanksgiving, present your requests to God" (Phil 4:6). By submitting to the bondage of anxiousness, you allow doubt to interfere with faith. Anxiousness, like many other obstacles we are faced with, will be there. Just as the fear of death worried Esther, so will other great worries infest your life. However, notice that with the help of Mordecai, Esther did not allow this worry to dictate her decision. Doubt was present, yet it was not a detriment to Esther in going forth to make the right decision in the sight of the Lord. Some people allow doubt to interfere with the will of God. Try your best to not become one of these individuals.

An example from the Bible that involves a man needing exponentially more help is the story of Jonah. Jonah was burdened with so much fear and doubt that he caused God to create a new connotation of the word *help*. The Lord had asked Jonah to serve him in going to speak to the people in the land of Nineveh. This was much too high of a request in Jonah's opinion, so he deliberately took a ship to a land called Tarshish—at least he attempted to. In this epic fish tale, God shows how far he will go in order to prove that his will shall be done. Jonah was thrown off of the side of the ship that he attempted to escape in and swallowed by a great fish prepared by God. He spent three days and three nights in the belly of the fish to reconsider carrying out the will of God. Jonah was not eager to preach against the wickedness of Nineveh. Jonah bargained that they would not listen to him but rather reject his efforts. Once Jonah was spit out by the great fish, however, he wasted no time in traveling to Nineveh! "Jonah began by going a day's journey into the city, proclaiming, 'forty more days and Nineveh will be overthrown'" (Jon 3:4). Can you imagine traveling a three-day journey on foot in one day? This journey had an unnatural kind of motivation behind it. It was a supernatural motivation; namely, the hand of God.

The learning curve varies among those who are asked to carry out God's will. This is a responsibility for all believers. No believers are excused from being charged with seeking God's will in their lives. This responsibility was inherited along with inheriting the love of Christ and eternal life. Be mindful of the fact that the Lord's will shall be done regardless of our feelings toward it. Building a solid foundation of faith is the cornerstone of being in stride with God. Falling away toward our own bets or expectations leaves us desolate as believers. God will turn away from those who deliberately turn away from him. Remembering that it's not about you; God will carry you much further and faster than will the lessening of faith. Going in your own direction disappoints the Lord.

SELF-SABOTAGE
When we tend to our own desires, leaving God out of the picture, it is the path to utter destruction.

Now this is what the Lord Almighty says: give careful thought to your ways. You have planted much, but have harvested little. You eat, but never have enough. You drink, but never have your fill. You put on clothes, but are not warm. You earn wages, but only to put them in a purse with holes in it. This is what the Lord Almighty says: give careful thoughts to your ways. Go up into the mountains and bring down timber and build the house, so that I may take pleasure in it and be honored, says the Lord. You expected much, but see, it turned out to be little. What you brought home, I blew away. Why? Declares the Lord Almighty. Because of my house, which remains a ruin, while each of you is busy with his own house. Therefore, because of you the heavens have withheld their dew and the earth its crops. (Hg 1:5–10)

Storing up your own interests and excluding God's say-so is the most dangerous thing a believer can do. I pray that this message does not fall upon deaf ears because the trouble that can be avoided is massive. It is a wise thing to learn from your own mistakes, but I consider it much wiser to learn from the mistakes of others. The Bible has an ocean of examples of mistakes made by others. Wisdom is gained in reading the Bible to remind us of the many shortcomings others have had to suffer God's discipline for. Society is consistently troubled with the idea of faith. From watching many atheist versus Christian debates, the most persistent issue in debating whether or not God is real is the issue of hard evidence. The Christian side of the debate ultimately relies on faith, while the atheist side of debates contrarily rests on hard evidence. The atheists are primarily saying "show me," while the Christians point to some logical and philosophical points but ultimately to the power of faith. Faith is required of believers the world over because it is the bridge to fulfilling our eternal gift of salvation.

SUSPICION DISMISSED

But there isn't much need for suspicion if you consider what Peter writes to us in 2 Peter. Peter, who was one of the twelve disciples that walked with Jesus, writes to us, "We did not follow cleverly invented stories when we told you about the power and coming of our Lord Jesus Christ, but we were *eyewitnesses* of his majesty. For he received honor and glory from God the Father when the voice came to him from the majestic glory, saying, this is my son whom I love; with him I am well pleased. We ourselves heard this voice that came from heaven when we were with him on the sacred mountain" (2 Pt 1:16–18, emphasis mine). Peter was mindful enough to include these powerful statements of truth to help believers and nonbelievers alike to bridge the gap.

Society has put into place a system of accountability: the witness system. In a court of law, there shall be witnesses to provide more stability to the story or stories being told in the courtroom. As citizens of the world, we accept this process. What Peter did for us who were not living during the time Jesus walked the earth was provide documentation as an eyewitness to the truth of the power manifest in Jesus Christ. He tells us that he was there! Peter assures us that the disciples were not following cleverly told stories, but real-life endeavors detectable with the human senses.

When a paramedic has a patient that decides he or she would not like to be transported to the hospital, the patient's signature of refusal must be recorded as well as a witness's signature. The witness's signature does exactly what the name implies: the witness serves as an extra person to confirm that that particular patient is in good enough condition and has the mental competency to refuse treatment and/or transport from the paramedics. Peter serves as this witness. Allow Peter's account to alleviate the moments of doubt we all have from time to time as humans. Doubt is a natural fear to have, for we are only human. Don't get trapped in the darkness of doubt, but rather persevere in reading the Bible, and enter a state of prayer. It's in the times of fear and doubt that God is yearning to be called upon.

OUR WEAKNESS IS STRENGTH

Paul tells us that when he is weak, he is actually strong, for the strength of Christ is made perfect in our weakness. 2 Corinthians 12:9–10 reads, "But he said to me, my grace is sufficient for you, for my power is made perfect in weakness. Therefore I will boast all the more gladly about my weaknesses, so that Christ's power may rest on me. That is why for Christ's sake, I delight in weaknesses, in insults, in hardships, in persecutions, in difficulties. For when I am weak, then I am strong." Faith is such a controversial subject because it requires belief in something that is not detected by the eyes or heard audibly with the ear. God was kind enough to leave his work in front of our eyes and made himself audible to our ears. Think of the earth and all of its splendor. The trees sway back and forth as the gusts of wind move them. The multitudes of animals, including the ones we have yet to discover deep down in the ocean, are so unique and intriguing. The abundance of different plants that fill the earth crowds our lives with sweet serenity. Nature is a magical artwork constructed by God's talented hand, only this is not a painting that he simply concocted with the stroke of a brush—it's much more complex than that.

ARTISTS LEAVE BEHIND THEIR ART

When I was in the fifth grade, I was fortunate enough to be a part of the junior docent experience given to students at my school via the gifted program. In my hometown of Saint Petersburg, Florida, there is a museum for the surrealist artist Salvador Dali. This artist is known for the elaborate stories told by the many pieces of artwork he created. The signature of his work is the irrational juxtaposition of two or more images. I was fascinated by all of the interesting stories each painting told, not to mention the prolific creativity this artist was able to capture in a mural. His surreal artwork will literally baffle you while you try to figure out just how he was able to pull the schemes of color and shape placement so perfectly to make multiple images appear inside of one grand image. This experience was one that gave me great gratification because as a fifth grader, being able to interpret the story of the painting in a new way gave me great joy. Here I was enlightening people about an amazing artist. What Salvador Dali had to show for his life was his artwork—his spectacular, fascinating surrealism. I think of the parallel an artist has with God. By faith, we believe that an artist once existed due to his or her artwork still in existence to behold. Therefore, should we not have faith in the Lord that he is very alive and in complete existence? The earth, man, and all of creation are pieces of artwork constructed by the hand of God—the artist. Do not be naive, friends! Just as the artist is known by the artwork he leaves behind, we know that God is among us by his creation. By the way, it did not take convincing the visitors at the museum that it was indeed Dali who made the paintings. Open your eyes and look around you to the majestic creations the good Lord has blessed us with. Realize that we walk by the power of faith in many circumstances, not just religion. Any time you make a decision, there is at least a morsel of faith injected into the decision because there are always unknown variables on the other side of making a commitment.

For instance, let's put marriage on the platform for evaluation. When two romantics enjoy one another's company enough while dating, it is not uncommon for the two to pursue the idea of marriage. When these two persons decide to take the legal action of getting married, faith is ever present in this life-altering commitment. Is faith not required when trusting each other to abstain from breaking the agreed-upon contract of marriage? Of course faith is present! There is no way of knowing what life will be like with that particular individual thirty years down the road. The implementation of faith is incurred in every instance of marriage. It is necessary to have faith in the unknown because humans simply cannot see beyond tomorrow. We have past statistics that can suggest what may occur in the future in certain circumstances, but no definite answer can be concluded.

DINOSAURS

A prominent concern in the world of atheism and deism is the concern of dinosaurs not being in the Bible. On the contrary, I'd like to point out the creature called Behemoth that is mentioned in the Bible. In the book of Job, while God is having words with Job, God says, "Look at Behemoth, which I made along with you and which feeds on grass like an ox. What strength it has in its loins, what power in the muscles of its belly! Its tail sways like a cedar; the sinews of its thighs are close knit. Its bones are tubes of bronze, its limbs like rods of iron. It ranks first among the works of God, yet its maker can approach it with the sword" (Jb 40:15–19). The beast named Behemoth mentioned in the Bible is often compared to a hippo or an elephant. But in verse 17, God says that Behemoth's tail sways like a cedar. A cedar tree does not call to mind a thin tail. The only creature's tail that fits this description is a dinosaur. Some may argue that the description says also that Behemoth eats grass like an ox. If we dissect this argument, it does not stand firm. Who's to say that this beast, Behemoth, though gigantic, had to be a meat eater? Even the dinosaurs we have learned are carnivores like the Tyrannosaurus Rex cannot be fully proven to be carnivores just because they had sharp teeth and Hollywood depicts them as monstrous terrorizers. Face value is a very fickle foundation to base a belief off of. Just because something is depicted one way does not make it fact.

HOPE

Faith in God's promises is what should drive all of us to persevere. The book of Romans tells us, "For in this hope we were saved. But hope that is seen is no hope at all. Who hopes for what he already has? But if we hope for what we do not yet have, we wait for it patiently" (Rm 8:24–25). There are two very strong reasons to have faith in the Lord. Faith in God means life has a purpose.

In the emergency medical systems district that I work in, twenty-four hours is the length of the shifts paramedics and firemen work. On one particular shift, I performed a forty-eight hour shift between two stations. Once my first twenty-four hour shift was done, I gathered my belongings to travel over to the second station where my shift would be completed. Mind you, these two stations were considered the busiest stations in the County of Manatee, which meant nonstop action around the clock. Fortunately, around midnight my partner and I were able to lie down for a couple of hours. This was not my normal partner due to me taking on the extra twenty-four hours of overtime. We were both worn down considerably from the day's work, and we knew it was not over just yet. In the serene darkness of that station bunk room, I lay pondering the ways of the Lord Almighty and felt moved to stir up discussion. Breaking the calming silence, my question shot across the room, "What do you think happens to us when we die?" My partner, seemingly a bit startled at the randomness, shot back, "What?" Again I raised the question in the midst of the bunk room darkness, "What do you think happens to us when we die?" My partner turned over toward me and gave me his reply, "I think we hit the dirt, and that is all." Intrigued yet let down by his response, my next question was, "Well, don't you believe in God?" He answered, "You know, I feel as though God is something society has made up to make ourselves feel better about the end to come. I think the reasoning behind the creation of God by people is to do just that, though for many of us it only makes us feel worse." So I proceeded to ask him what he felt life's purpose was, and he told me that his opinion was that life's purpose is to live well, make your mark on the earth, and then it's all over. He let out a long, drawn-out yawn, turning back over to attempt to fall asleep.

The take-home point to learn from this story is that it's not about you. Living well, making your mark on earth, becoming successful, etc. are all great achievements, but when they are your only focal points, you have missed out on what was most important—God. To believe that life's purpose is all about you is not what God intended; in fact it is in complete opposition to what Jesus tells us in saying "love one another." Faith in God is monumental because it provides purpose. Without purpose, humans are mere leaves, going in whatever direction the wind is moving. How depressing of a thought is that to believe that we are all just here floating from one place to the next? What would be the sense in a world created for people to sway from one direction to the next without cause? The Bible tells us that our purpose is to love one another and follow God's commands. As opposed to what numerous people believe, this is not a life we were given to live with the idea that we only live once. We were endowed with the choice to live once, but more importantly, we were glorified with the divine grace to live forever!

The second important factor that faith in God presents is the necessity of morality. Without faith in the Lord, or further, the simple belief in the Lord, ethics would be obsolete. There would be no need for practicing ethics in life because sin would be a nonexistent enterprise. Condemnation would then only be an imaginary matter to either accept or reject based off of feelings. Speaking of feelings, you cannot trust feelings because they are not in stride with the way of the Spirit. The Bible tells us that the Spirit is in contrast with the flesh (feelings) so that we cannot do what we *feel*. Atheists will proclaim to have no faith in anything, but with all due respect, I'm here to disprove that fallacy. To not believe in anything at all takes just as much faith, if not more faith, than to believe in God. A great verse about faith comes from 1 Peter: "Though you have not seen him, you love him; and even though you do not see him now, you believe in him and are filled with an inexpressible and glorious joy, for you are receiving the end result of your faith, the salvation of your souls" (1 Pt 1:8–9). Readers, allow that last part of the verse to marinate for a second. Expand your vision enough to keep in mind the result of what having faith brings into fruition. Life is good, but the conservation of your soul trumps any matter or worry in life you may have, for the matters of the world are only temporary.

Think of life as a trial run for the real deal in eternity. Our lives now are precursors to unending happiness in heaven if we can just hold on long enough through our faith in Christ until our time has lapsed here on earth. The Bible instructs us also to not love the things of this world for this very reason: it will not last. For the person who has doubt in his or her heart about faith in God, I would like to tell you the key lies in having faith. The key to faith in God is to walk with him. Faith in the Lord is not meant to be a stationary, inactive gift. Faith is meant to be active in our everyday endeavors. Praying with faith while living out God's commands is the best way to grow in your faith. Blessings are brought to the faithful, and faithfulness is measured by God through our actions as well as the condition of our hearts. One of the minor prophets, Hosea, was tested in faith in probably the most eccentric way God has ever tested a servant's faith. What God did to test Hosea's faith was clearly out of the norm. Hosea is considered to be a minor prophet because of the length of book he wrote was shorter in length, not because his work was of any less significance. The people of God had been unfaithful to him, unfaithful like prostitutes. Displeased with the people before him, God instructed the prophet Hosea to go find a harlot named Gomer and marry her. This woman was unfaithful, as a harlot would be expected to be, and left Hosea for another man. However, even after she was loved by another man and eventually put up for sale as a slave, God commanded the prophet Hosea to love his wife Gomer once again! The book of Hosea reads, "The Lord said to me, go, show your love to your wife again, though she is loved by another and is an adulteress. Love her as the Lord loves the Israelites, though they turn to other gods and love the sacred raisin cakes. So I bought her for fifteen shekels of silver and about a homer and a lethek of barley. Then I told her, you are to live with me many days; you must not be a prostitute or be intimate with any man, and I will live with you" (Hos 3:1–3). The name *Hosea* means "salvation," which is what the Lord intended for his message to be to Israel. Hosea was an amazingly faithful servant to the Lord.

Another peculiar action carried out by the Lord was with the prophet Ezekiel. Idolatry had taken place in the people of Israel's temple, and idolatry had become the delight of their eyes. As God's servant, Ezekiel was to suffer the loss of the delight of his eyes just as the people of Israel would lose the temple they defiled. "The word of the Lord came to me: Son of Man, with one blow I'm about to take away from you the delight of your eyes. Yet do not lament or weep or shed any tears. Groan quietly; do not mourn for the dead. Keep your turban fastened and your sandals on your feet; do not cover the lower part of your face or eat the customary food of mourners. So I spoke to the people in the morning, and in the evening my wife died. The next morning I did as I had been commanded" (Ez 24:15–18). The mention of these two prophets with uncomfortable trials is to reflect the power of faith they possessed when faced with adversity. In the end, it all worked out for the salvation and growth in spirit for the people of Israel, as it always does.

God is the great orchestra conductor that you see in the front of the musicians directing them to stay on cue with the right rhythm and sound. We, his chosen people, are those musicians playing instruments under his command. God is in control. As loyal servants, our mission is to follow his lead via faith, and we will not be led astray. God is faithful, loving us more and more as we follow his divine will. Wherever you are at this time in your life, remember to lean always on the Lord, having faith forever.

CHAPTER 4

SIGNS FROM ABOVE

IN THIS CHAPTER, I WILL provide for you many indications of God's existence via the signs that he leaves us. First, we will begin with the signs from the Bible that have already been recorded for us to review. Later, I will reveal to you some amazing signs of his existence God has shown me in my personal life. My prayer is that you absorb and retain my personal experiences to strengthen your faith. It is a wonderful thing to be able to share spiritual experiences when God blesses his followers with them. God does not exactly extend the same type of signs as he did in such days of the Old Testament in terms of flooding the earth or parting the Red Sea, but he does make his presence known.

SHARE YOUR TESTIMONY

I'd like to encourage you to share your testimony in your church congregation when given the opportunity; this is a great form of witnessing that is a primary purpose for followers of Christ. We are to bring those that are in the darkness to the light by our gifts, lifestyles, and personal experiences. All of these are gifts from God to shine as a brighter light of truth to the masses. Don't allow shyness or minor stage fright to conceal God's glory because you never know who is in the gathering that can benefit from your life. Sometimes, hearing another individual tell his or her testimony is all a person needs who may be going through the same exact situation or a similar one in nature. We all go through rough patches in life, so explaining how God saw you through your struggle can serve as a troubleshooting guide to help the next soul longing for relief from a closely related issue.

One person got up at my home church and told how he fell into temptation after being raised correctly in a Christian home and made it through the consequences by the grace of God alone. He explained to the congregation how he lost sight of what was sound doctrine in his life, backsliding into a dark hole, what I would call that corridor that lies between an individual's greatness and insanity. He told us of how he went off to Bible college to study the Word of God, only to be kicked out for insubordination. His comment was geared toward the fallacy of Christian college being completely ethical after explaining how the college gave him the boot. His words were, "You think when you're at a Christian college, everyone is going to behave as a Christian...Not the case." Once he got back to his hometown, he got involved in a business that was performing illegal acts; namely money laundering. I cannot recall all of the charges this gentleman was facing, but I do remember that he relayed to us the powerful message that God delivered him from five felony charges by pure grace. His urgent comment was, "You think you are out here alone and happen to come across some good luck at times...until you realize that it had to be God's hand at work."

This gentleman told us that he ran from the Lord in the opposite direction for a few years at a time, the longest stint being seven years. However, the most important piece of information this man provided for us was the message that *God never forsakes you*. Even after he ran for years at a time, God never rejected him when he repented and longed to come back home to his heavenly Father's cloak of protection. God rescued him from the jaws of prison time. Now this gentleman is the chaplain for a Division I university in the athletics department. His joy was radiating throughout the church when he revealed the gratification his career has brought him. He even had the opportunity to be the chaplain for Team USA in soccer during the World Cup!

DON'T WASTE YOUR TIME

Getting caught up in the corridor of confusion consumes precious time in your life. Productivity is squelched by the deceiving grasp sin can have on your life. Understand that tolerating the leeching effects of operating in this corridor of discombobulation is only keeping you from God's greatness. With the help of Christ, delivery can be made possible from any circumstances. God answers our prayers, giving us what we need when he feels the time is right and we are ready for it. Get away from the thought process of thinking that it's all about you, because it's not. It's all about him. His glory. His purposes. His will. Adapt your prayer life toward what God wants for your life, not what you would have for your life. God knows the desires we have, and according to the Bible, the Lord longs to give them to us, but under his plans only. Life is not about getting everything you want, though it would be nice.

SIGNS FROM THE BIBLE

Let's take a look at the signs God has left for all to witness through his holy book. I'm sure you've seen a rainbow in the sky at some point. This is a sign from God that he would never again flood the earth. God made this promise to Noah and left a rainbow to serve as his signature on that covenant he made.

And God said, this is the sign of the covenant I am making between me and you and every living creature with you, a covenant for all generations to come. I have set my rainbow in the clouds, and it will be the sign of the covenant between me and the earth. Whenever I bring clouds of the earth and the rainbow appears in the clouds, I will remember my covenant between me and you [Noah] and all living creatures of every kind. Never again will the waters become a flood to destroy all life. Whenever the rainbow appears in the clouds, I will see it and remember the everlasting covenant between God and all living creatures of every kind on the earth. So God said to Noah, this is the sign of the covenant I have established between me and all life on the earth. (Gn 9:12–17)

The rainbow in the sky is a way God is communicating to us one of his promises. God chose to punish the world in different ways, as we see in the Old Testament. When Hezekiah became ill to the point of impending death, he wept and prayed to the Lord. God heard Hezekiah's prayers and decided to shoot him a message via the prophet Isaiah: "Go back unto Hezekiah, the ruler of my people, this is what the Lord, the God of your father David says: I have heard your prayers and seen your tears; I will heal you. On the third day from now you will go up to the temple of the Lord. I will add fifteen years to your life. And I will deliver you and the city from the hand of the king of Assyria. I will defend this city for my sake and for the sake of my servant David" (2 Kgs 20:5–6). A sign, which we often feel the longing for, is validation from the Lord, whether it be answered prayer, a dream, etc. Hezekiah also wanted reassurance of this message spoken from the prophet Isaiah. Hezekiah questioned how he would discern if the sign was from God. What would serve as a sign? "Isaiah answered, 'this is the Lord's sign to you that the Lord will do what he has promised: shall the shadow go forward ten steps, or shall it go back ten steps'? It is a simple matter for the shadow to go forward ten steps, said Hezekiah. Rather, have it go back ten steps. Then the prophet Isaiah called on the Lord and the Lord made the shadow go back the ten steps it had gone down on the stairway of Ahaz" (2 Kgs 20:9–11). Here we read how God left Hezekiah an amazing sign that he would heal Hezekiah's illness. God vowed to add fifteen years to Hezekiah's life after hearing his weeping in prayer. The Lord shows compassion to those that cry out to him. God shows the utmost pity and empathy on those that are willing to cry out to him in prayer, not holding back what's on their hearts.

In the Bible, God is constantly molding the Israelites for greatness. He also has to discipline Israel on a regular basis, but always for their own good in his divine purposes. A tremendous example of this is when Joshua governed the Israelites. Joshua was Moses's successor. There was a fierce battle going on between the Amorites and the Israelites, and Joshua interceded with legendary bravado. "On the day the Lord gave the Amorites over to Israel, Joshua said to the Lord in the presence of Israel: Sun, stand still over Gibeon, and you, moon, over the Valley of Aijalon. So the sun stood still, and the moon stopped, till the nation avenged itself on its enemies, as it is written in the book of Jashar. The sun stopped in the middle of the sky and delayed going down about a full day. There has never been a day like it before or after, a day when the Lord listened to a human being. Surely the Lord was fighting for Israel!" (Jo 10:12–14). We see that God can communicate to us in multiple ways as we look to recorded history in the Bible.

The prophet Gideon was sent to help the Israelites. Gideon performed a unique test to measure whether or not the Lord called him. Sure enough, it was in fact God speaking to Gideon. Gideon's test was the process of taking a rag and placing it on the ground to see if God would fill it with dew by morning but leave the surrounding ground dry. God indeed filled Gideon's rag with dew but left the ground around it dry. Then, Gideon requested that God fill the surrounding ground—everything but the rag—with dew. Just as God answered Gideon's first request for a sign, he also answered the second request: "That night God did so. Only the fleece was dry; all the ground was covered with dew" (Jgs 6:40). God both answers supernaturally and in more conventional ways.

YOUR VALUE

A message I'd respectfully like to extend to the reader is to avoid becoming worthless in the sight of the Lord. This is a bold statement, yes, but it is not to be taken offensively. No one on this entire universe is worthless unless that person chooses to be. There are two different kinds of value when it comes to the merit of our lives. The first kind of value—and most significant kind of value, might I add—is godly value. Godly worth should be every Christian's first priority in life. Godly value is measured by God by how well we follow his commands, lead lives of Christian example, study the Lord's Word, and so forth. God is proud of us when we make great achievements. God is proud of us when we receive earthly rewards from our hard work. However, what impresses our heavenly Father the most is the spiritual maturity we possess as his children. The Lord wants to know ultimately how well we know his Son, Jesus Christ. He also wants to know what we are doing to spread the Gospel, or the good news.

The second type of value someone holds is earthly value. In the world we live in, a worthy person is often depicted in the media as the person who has wealth, beauty, and fame. This school of thought is a matter of having been brainwashed and losing sight of truth. True value in an individual is more so internal than external. The internal, referring to character, ethical code, and spiritual beliefs, is what God looks at. The external, evaluated by men, refers to wealth, beauty, and fame. All of the externals are great, but notice that all of the externals have a common downfall: they fade. A unique example provided in the Bible on the subject of worthlessness is the sign God gave Jeremiah using a linen belt. In the book of Jeremiah, the Lord uses a simple article of clothing to make his divine point.

This is what the Lord said to me: go and buy a linen belt and put it around your waist, but do not let it touch water. So I bought a belt, as the Lord directed, and put it around my waist. Then the word of the Lord came to me a second time: take the belt you bought and are wearing around your waist, and go now to Perath and get the belt I told you to hide there. So I went to Perath and dug up the belt and took it from the place where I had hidden, but now was ruined and completely useless...These wicked people, who refuse to listen to my words, they follow the stubbornness of their hearts and go after other gods to serve and worship them, will be like this belt—completely useless! (Jer 13:1–7, 10)

The result of the people of Judah and Jerusalem was divine discipline, for these nations had become full of pride to the point that they were ineffectual in the eyes of the Lord. The pride of life is the downfall of the individual seeking God; the two are not able to coexist because God takes delight in a humble spirit. Signs from above are strong indicators that the Lord is watching each of our lives intently. The Lord tests those who he loves. When a divine sign is revealed to an individual, he or she must take heart and begin to search out what God's message is for him or her. The Bible is a manual and is overall probably the greatest sign of God *from* God. The Bible instructs us how to properly handle the issues of the earth effectively in stride. We don't always feel strongly about how God may say to go about doing things, but his Holy Word, when studied, irrefutably leads us to greener pastures.

A MEDICAL STORY: SIGNS VERSUS SYMPTOMS

In the medical field, I evaluate many patients. The array of patients covers a broad spectrum of illnesses. Likewise, there are various amounts of traumatic injuries that can occur in a patient. I respond to diabetics, epilepsy patients, stroke patients, heart attacks, obstetric patients, and a vast amount of other patients. Every call holds a new adventure. In paramedic school, one of the first skills I learned when assessing a patient was to know the signs of the patient's condition as opposed to the patient's symptoms. The difference between a sign and a symptom is a matter of the first being objective and the other subjective. If you are to call 911 because you had the worst headache of your life, which is often a symptom of a stroke, while at the same time you felt extremely nauseous, my crew and I would come assess you and makes notes of those findings, or *symptoms*. Symptoms are subjective, or in other words, findings that only the patient can feel or express. Now if I were to assess your blood pressure, palpate your pulse, or feel your skin temperature, these findings would be called *objective* because I can see or come to these conclusions on my own accord—these findings are referred to as *signs*. If you notice the subtle difference between the two, you will quickly come to find that one is more of an inward manifestation versus the other being an outward manifestation.

There is a parallel in the sector of signs and symptoms to be compared to with the life of a believer. As chosen children of God, it is our sole duty to live our lives to reflect the characteristics of Jesus Christ. When we have Jesus in our hearts and feel his love, this would be termed a *symptom* in the medical field because this is an inward manifestation that a believer would have to describe or convey. The challenge posed to Christians is that we lead lives that give off *signs* to unbelievers. An unbeliever should be able to identify us by the way we choose to conduct ourselves as well as the way we choose *not* to conduct ourselves. Violence, slander, maliciousness, and the like are negative signs that won't likely be deemed as the behavior of a Christian. Inversely, love, kindness, and steadfast patience are positive signs of an upright Christian. No one is perfect, and by no means should anyone expect to be the happiest of all people simply because he or she is a believer. However, gentleness and persistent empathy are iconic attributes we should strive to display.

BAPTISM: AN OUTWARD SIGN

Another outward sign of all Christians is the divine event of baptism. In Mark 16:16, Jesus says, "Whoever believes and is baptized will be saved, but whoever does not believe will be condemned." Then in John 3:5, Jesus tells Nicodemus how he can be born again when Nicodemus questions how a man can be born again when he is old: "Jesus answered, I tell you the truth no one can enter the kingdom of God unless he is born of water and the spirit. Flesh gives birth to flesh, but the spirit gives birth to the spirit. You should not be surprised at my saying, you must be born again." I urge you to become baptized if you have not been already. Baptism is a criterion for your salvation according to scripture. I can remember my youth pastor teaching my youth group the importance of becoming saved and why baptism was so pertinent. His words were, "Baptism is an outward sign of an inward commitment!"

COMMUNITY

Get involved in your local Christian community. You might find that being in the midst of other believers will increase the strength of your walk. Attending church service, small groups, and other activities such as international mission trips are some ideas to get you started. I enjoyed my youth group days; my youth pastor was animated along with his wife. This was a perfect fit for the middle school students and high school students alike. Having a goofy, easy-going pastoral staff made everyone more comfortable because there wasn't the usual dry, serious approach to the Gospel that usually goes beyond adolescents' attention. On select weekends, we would have the opportunity to participate in unconventional team games like broom ball, which is basically the game of ice hockey played with brooms and a ball instead of hockey sticks and a puck. Imagine a stampede of youth students scurrying across the ice at full speed after a ball with very minimal ability to stop! It was a blast, and was a lot more wholesome of an activity to indulge in as well as fellowship with other like-minded Christians.

Fellowshipping with like-minded people is so conducive to spiritual growth. When the company you surround yourself with is pure and headed in a positive direction, the characteristics tend to rub off on you, especially during the years of puberty and adolescence—a time of vulnerability to all sorts of influence. It was sound counsel that brought me to be the person that I am today. The *retention* of the counsel was left up to me.

Please don't be one of the zombies in church who attend because they were cornered into going or because it just seemed like the right thing to do. My young nephew attends church with me from time to time; he was one of the zombies in attendance before I challenged him to actively retain the message from each sermon. Paying full attention to the message tends to be most difficult for younger people, but we've all had that sermon where we did not get enough sleep and the air conditioning breezes across us just right with a whisper that says "close your eyes." In today's time, it's never been more convenient to attend church. For the lazy bums such as my sister (I say that jokingly), some churches broadcast live sermons online, allowing you to watch from the comfort of your own couch or even your bed! There've been countless times when I've called my sister up with the invitation to attend church, and she politely lets me know that she will be viewing the service from her home. I try to coax her into attending in person with me, explaining that it's all the more enlightening and natural to sit in the pews. My attempts are heard, yet they do not succeed. All in all, the message is by far the most critical thing to retain.

Small groups are wonderful addendums to worship. Churches instill small groups in the curriculum to allow members to fellowship with the other Christians in the same church. This goes back to the piece of advice that was given earlier about the company you keep. Small groups are perfect for bouncing ideas off of like-minded people all studying a topic from scripture. Interpretation of scripture can be confusing, so when having a larger foundation studying the exact same thing, the difficulty is disseminated among the team of readers rather than falling on one person. Aside from the studying portion, small groups are good for other personal needs that we have. I can remember plenty of times when people needed to vent or talk about other important events going on in their lives. Also, if everyone comes to an agreement, hors d'oeuvres and drinks are big crowd pleasers because let's face it—who's going to reject food and beverages? One year, my parents' small group decided to host a Super Bowl party! Christians need all the support and backup they can get—and don't forget it. The secular style of living is by no means scarce as soon as you walk out of your front door. It's present when changing the channels on the television set, heard on the radio while driving in the car, and overheard in conversations while jogging the trail in the park. Spiritual warfare isn't going to subside; therefore Christians must be properly guarded in all aspects.

CHAPTER 5
LONE WOLF/SIGN NUMBER ONE

HAVE YOU EVER FELT LIKE the outcast? I have. My natural personality never exactly fit the mold of a conformist. I always enjoyed socializing with friends and such, but my alone time was equally satisfying. Isolation had always been a remedy from the fast-paced flow of society moving to and fro. To bask in the abundance of silence that solitude brought me served as therapy; it restored the balance to the confusion of everyday life. Apart from the joys isolation brought me through peaceful reflection, individuality was among my top character traits—at least this is what I strive for it to be. My ambition is to never become a burden to anyone, longing only to be an invited addition to any group or establishment. The words *bear your own weight* were engraved in me, for I agreed with the statement wholeheartedly from the day I learned it.

It helped immensely having a father who taught me just the same. Just about every break from school that my brother and I got, my father would have us both out in the yard pulling weeds, mowing the grass, trimming trees, and things of this nature. We painted on multiple occasions, took on projects involving vehicle repair, and handled all sorts of domestic projects. My mother enjoyed having outside work done, though the domestic missions we took on such as painting, laying new, polished wood flooring down, and more left a more infatuated glimmer in my mother's eye. My father, who was both an engineer and schoolteacher for many years, fully understood what hard work meant. He would consistently tell my younger brother and me how he had grown up in a large household where his brothers and he grew their strength from hauling sizable tree limbs out in a field. My father's intent with having my younger brother and me keep busy during school breaks was to build character. At the time we dreaded the thought of giving up our precious breaks to become intimate with grass and weeds. Even during the periods when school was in session, my father made sure that my brother and I were involved in sports or some form of extracurricular activity. He was adamant about keeping us busy, wearing us down with every opportunity available—and for good reason. He explained to us that it was better to be involved in things rather than to have idle time on our hands to get into mischief. My understanding of the meaning of holding a strong work ethic was potent with the measures my father took. We were required to apply ourselves wherever we could.

Something tells me that my dad learned this from the previous children he had over the years. There were eleven of us in all, my brother and me being number ten and number eleven. My brother inquired about the reasoning behind my father's decision to have so many children by asking him one day, "Dad, why did you have so many kids?" My dad replied, "Do you think I should have stopped before I got to you?" Dad always had a witty response prepared. So the work ethic was concrete within my bones, and I knew from a very early age that work was a big portion of life itself. I also learned from a very early age that there were typically two categories of individuals in the world. These two categories are leaders and followers, or conformists and nonconformists. Please do not be misled by the often misplaced confusion of a person who follows the rules versus a rule breaker. Being a nonconformist does not mean that you are a rebel; it just means that you are strong willed in your beliefs. The utmost pioneering precedent was Jesus Christ. His entire life was nonconformity at its finest! Other models of nonconformists include Dr. Martin Luther King Jr., Gandhi, and Abraham Lincoln, to name a few other cases. If you ever have trouble deciding which of the two categories you personally fit in, be aware that there is absolutely nothing wrong with either.

But there is one valid fact that I wish to unveil. Look to the fact that Jesus Christ, our own Lord and savior, was a nonconformist. Truthfully, all Christians have inadvertently chosen the path of the nonconformist by choosing to be saved. Think about Jesus Christ's early life, his actions, and what each of his actions stood for. The majority of the world chose the way of sinful nature, while Jesus chose a perfect life lived to God's standards in order to cleanse us of our sins. The book of Romans provides enlightening advice for nonconformity: "And do not be *conformed* to this world, but be transformed by the renewing of your mind, so that you may prove what the will of God is, that which is good and acceptable and perfect" (Rm 12:2, emphasis mine). In 1 John 2:15–17, the Bible instructs us, "Do not love the world with the things in the world. If anyone loves the world, the love of the Father is not in him. For all that is in the world—the desires of the flesh and the desires of the eyes and pride and possessions—is not from the Father but is from the world. And the world is passing away along with its desires, but whoever does the will of God abides forever." Heed the instruction that lies within the text of John. The reward is everlasting. The devil's magical mirage of earthly pleasures is weak, with artificial foundations. The deceptive reasoning for loving this world as Satan does is a lie. Do not build foundations upon this; Jesus assures us that he alone is the truth, the way, and the light, according to John 14:6. Trust in him to find that you won't be disappointed or let down. Have you ever anticipated something to come to fruition that simply did not measure up to your expectations? Trusting in the Lord with all your heart and mind is not an effort that will go unrewarded. It takes courage to oppose the masses. The path of the nonconformist is beset on all sides in the midst of spiritual warfare. The war for your mind and soul is an uphill battle; the swim is fought against the current. The marathon is run against the wind. Leadership is a gift of the righteous. We are endowed with the truth and are held accountable for living by it. The Bible tells us in Exodus, "Furthermore, you shall select out of all the people able men who fear God, men of truth, those who hate dishonest gain; and you shall place these over them as leaders of thousands, of hundreds, of fifties and of tens" (Ex 18:21). The best form of leadership is the art of servant leadership. "Do nothing from selfishness or empty conceit, but with humility of mind regard one another as more important than yourselves" (Phil 2:3). I encourage Christians to stand up as leaders for the glory of our God who is watching down on us intently, monitoring us in hopes of seeing righteousness catapult us into action. Consider what Proverbs tells us in regard to this: "Where there is no guidance the people fall, but in abundance of counselors, there is victory" (Prv 11:14). In our Congress, the head of leadership is of course the president of the United States. Below him there are subheads who help to govern as well. We know them by the regal titles of senator, governor, mayor, and the like. In churches, the head of the congregation is the senior pastor. The senior pastor is the lead man overseeing the subheads beneath him known as elders, deacons, and ushers. Take sports teams for an illustration. The coined captain of the team is the quarterback when it comes to football. But it takes a big group of people to effectively govern the team as a whole. The head coach, defensive coordinator, the offensive coordinator, and so forth: all these individuals play an instrumental role in leading the overall team to victory.

During fire academy, the chief of the academy worked with the council of lieutenants, captains, and administrative persons to effectively and properly govern my academy class. Among the thirty-five men that were students in my class, the fire instructors made squads, appointing each squad a squad captain. One standout was awarded the title of class president. His enthusiasm was uncanny in all things that pertain to the fire service. He arrived an entire hour before the start of class each day to raise the flag, being sure to police the grounds for trash and debris. On the days we had physical training, he would take on the leadership role of standing before the class and performing the particular exercise we were to do. While running, he would chant inspirational quotes and affirmations while the rest of us marveled at his leadership. This class president did not miss the essence of leadership skills either, maintaining the true form of servant leadership. His actions spoke louder than his deep voice in the way he performed servant leadership. He gave rides to those that needed them and studied with his squad more so than any other leader of other squads. He was bold enough to raise questions during lectures that others were too fearful of asking. Because of these ways he administered through his actions, he was honored by each of us.

CONFRONTATION

Conflict arose while I was working at my first career job with the fire department. Questions had been raised about me being what was perceived as standoffish. It began one early morning just after I had arrived at the station to check out the equipment. Instead of hanging out with the crew in the engine bay after the morning duties were performed, I chose to stay inside, seeking an alternate mission rather than the routine joke telling at 7:45 a.m. As I sat down reading at the dining room table inside of the station, a fellow fireman came in to offer a piece of advice. Placing his hand on my shoulder, the fire medic advised, "You know, Hogans, it would probably be a much better idea for you to come on out and hang with the guys, otherwise they may think negatively of you." I looked up at him, acknowledging his advice. He then continued, "That's just the way firemen think here." With a polite head nod, I fell into deep thought. Very rarely had I been cautioned in this way and told to join a group. The thought of not being accepted on a social level was not an issue, but to think that I may be chastised or patronized because of my laid-back nature sounded absurd. It was almost as if the gentleman was giving me an opaque ultimatum to hang out with them—or else. It was this day and this experience that quickly showed me the peculiar truth that the fire department I was working at mirrored a fraternity. Fraternities, cliques, clubs, and the like were at the very bottom on my list of personal interests. The closest I had ever come to enrolling in one of these types of organizations in the past was a sport. Bowling teams, cross country, track teams, and soccer teams were the only things that had come close to a formal social group outside of my church family.

Near the end of my ten-week orientation, the training staff decided to take the probies out to eat. During this outing is where the second conflict arose, right there at the lunch table while I was eating hot wings. A fireman who will remain anonymous sat across from me at a long table that seated the ten new hires and about four or five training lieutenants. It was a splendid time there at the restaurant until a popular firefighting song came on that led to a wager. The fireman shot a piercing look along the entire table accompanied by a devious smile. He confidently began, "I'm willing to bet a hundred dollars to any of you probies that can guess the name of this song and the band!" Answers began to funnel in. The solemn grin was plastered on the firemen's face, exuding pure confidence that none of the newbies would guess the song in a million years. I filed through the list of possibilities in my head. Older bands were not foreign to me because my father's music over the years equipped me quite well. Upon the band's name reaching the tip of my tongue, I urgently expelled the words from my mouth. "The Ohio Players!" I announced. His grin turned stale following my remark. Proceeding to go on with the business of finishing his lunch, it was apparent that he was joking about the hundred dollar wager. "What happened to the bet?" I asked playfully. He slowly looked up at me from his plate of food with a face of stone and said, "I'm not going to pay *you* a hundred dollars." Not realizing the threshold of anger he apparently exceeded, I joked once more. "Okay, I get it; this guy is a man of his word, I see." He whipped his head up at me; this time his face and ears had become flushed with redness. "I will take you outside and whoop your tail, boy!" The longtime fireman threatened. Holding my ground, I shot back, "You can try." He then reached into his back pocket for five twenty dollar bills and commanded I better not say one word to him ever again as he slapped the money on the table. I discreetly placed the bills into my wallet.

As soon as we got back to the drill grounds to conclude the second half of the training day, an officer requested me to come to his office. The fireman had made the overseeing officer aware that I had accepted the money that he facetiously gambled with. When it was all said and done, I was to give the money back, except for twenty dollars that he said I could keep. My next move was an apology to him because I sensed that he felt disrespected by me. We shook hands, giving one another a manly hug of respect to squash the feud. Little did I know that this particular occurrence would spread like wildfire throughout the department. Gossip seemed to be the way of the fire department that I was working with at the time. In fact it was a running joke and warning to conceal any personal information that you did not want to be widely known because individuals there spread information like a contagious disease. Never before did I feel as though I needed to be cautious in conversation. It was an eerie feeling to know and see firsthand that this spreading of rumors was fact. Employees from all over the department would stop me in my tracks to inquire about the heated confrontation I had been involved in. The assumption that the meeting allegedly resolving the issue would end in that office proved to be only naivety on my behalf. Conflict, at a time a probationary employee needed it to be absent, began to crescendo. Stakes had been raised, for eyes were monitoring my every move at this point in probation, heightening the necessity to perform above average. By the time the heat simmered down from this incident, the next obstacle awaited me at the next station in my rotation, which was known for giving probies a tough time. It was told to me that the crew at this particular station had even driven one new hire from their previous hiring group to write a letter to the city! On the first shift that I arrived at the station, the station captain extended the expectations to me, wasting no time at all. His main concern was that I learn the location of each and every piece of equipment on all four apparatuses. I thought this feat would take a good five shifts or so. I was baffled when the station captain tested me on my second shift. I only had a 50 percent success rate locating equipment. At the end of the month, as this was a regular evaluation span, the station captain gave me a subpar grading mark in *finding equipment*. Another captain questioned me about the reasoning behind the low grade on my monthly evaluation, and I explained to him that I did not have a sufficient amount of time to familiarize myself with each of the apparatuses.

The captain cut his eye at me and snapped, "Are you calling the other captain a liar?"

"No," I answered. "But he only gave me until the second shift to recognize each location and what that compartment contained." As he looked at me with a gaze of disgust, my intuition told me that he had marked me as one who casts blame on others. This just wasn't the case. Appalled at the title the captain had silently conveyed to me with his piercing eyes, my face emitted worry.

He fired at me, "Don't give me that look...Don't you give me that look." Silence filled the room, but there were audible loud sounds of disturbance blazing in my head. Progressing to my final station brought a sense of relief to the weight on my shoulders; the light at the end of the tunnel could be seen—or maybe it was a hallucination. From the moment I stepped foot in the station's door of my last rotation, a series of interrogating questions awaited me during my initial meeting with the station captain. From a functionality standpoint, this particular station was the finest. It performed marine rescues, including the use of a boat and a dive-oriented vehicle. Water rescue was their specialty, making for electrifying rescue calls out in the open gulf. Kayakers who were in distress, boaters who had flipped, and other water sport participants such as jet skiers were among the patients we rescued. The station itself was state of the art. Every station in the department was equipped with a gym, but this gym exceeded the rest.

I had a blue folder that held criteria for my probationary period, which was a full year in length. A requirement recorded in the list provided to me was the directive of making contact with the lieutenant of rescue on a monthly basis. My captain at the time sat down with me in his office and declared that he wanted me to keep a log of my monthly contacts with a printed piece of paper and pen. I was also to contact each one of my mentors assigned to me by the department and email him once the task was complete. He gave me about a week. I successfully completed all items on the list of tasks given to me by the captain, with one minor discrepancy in the documentation of contacting the lieutenant of rescue. It is true; I decided to be rogue in this situation, which was unacceptable. I thought it a small enough deviation to get by with to document the contact I made to the lieutenant of rescue via email; this way there would be no need for printing out a chart to record with pen or pencil. I emailed this captain the details of how my assignments were completed and the format in which I completed them. On the email system the department had, you could see whether or not the email had been read. The email was marked *read* by the captain no later than fifteen minutes from me sending it to him. With the electronic confirmation that the captain of my current station had read my email, I was at ease, having completed my assignments. To my surprise, the captain invited me into his office for discussion regarding an *incomplete assignment*. I was at a loss for words as I sat down before him, digesting the comment "I'm writing you up" that rolled off of his tongue. The lieutenant of rescue, seated directly next to me, was skillfully mute. I guess there had been a part of me that thought he would have spoken up for me in spite of him being somewhat of a component in the matter. The lieutenant of rescue, after all, was the person I had made my contacts with. But not a peep left his mouth; he had zoned out into another space and time—or so it seemed.

The workplace felt like a field of landmines; every shift I reported to duty brought about strange vibes. I felt no one was trying to be an advocate. There were select firemen who did what they could to help me through, though all the negativity clouded their efforts like a sunny day suddenly turning into dark stormy weather. During these catastrophic segments, my hope was laser-beam focused on prayer. Probation meant just that—probation. Knowing this, it was understood that if the fire department felt the need to cut me loose, the only thing between keeping and losing my job was the snap of the chief's fingers. As a probationary employee, I learned that I had no appeal rights in the employment contract. Also, the union all probies were recommended to join gave absolutely no representation for the probies, though I paid union dues. Work had become a mess. It did not help that early in the year I lost a radio on the fire grounds and missed the call-out parameters by two minutes when I called in sick for one shift. As a probationary employee, my file had three incidents reported total. My quietness around the station was not in my favor either; many of the firemen disliked that I was rather distant from the fold. Prayer was on the forefront of my mind. The department recalled the write-up regarding the lost radio and knocked it down to a lesser offense. Had it not, my three offenses collectively would have placed me in the *chronic offender* margin.

THE CROSS IN THE CORNER

Prayers continued to be sent up to God as I hoped for the best. Ultimately, I had not understood why things were going so badly; therefore I looked to God to show me a sign. Not only were matters at work a burden to behold, my romantic relationship with my girlfriend was deteriorating day by day. Mind you, my girlfriend was living with me at this time, a big no-no for Christians who are not married. My reasoning was that she was the one, and my plans were to marry her anyhow. On the way to work one morning, I turned off my radio and began to pray intently for the whole twenty-minute drive to work for a sign that God was with me through this gigantic battle I was in the middle of. My spirit became saturated with uncertainty, allowing confusion to infest my mental state. My verbiage during prayer on this particular morning included, "God...please show me a sign that you are on my side...Show me, Lord, that you are in my corner." I used the phrase "in my corner" to pay homage to what my situation felt like—being in a heated boxing ring. Parking my car, I walked briskly into the fire station. I still had on my civilian clothing because my uniforms were in my locker. I began to change into my uniform.

As I fastened my belt in the dressing room, my eyes suddenly fixated on a shiny silver cross resting in the corner of the room atop the counter. This was the same room I dressed in every shift, and I had never noticed the cross sitting in the corner before. My prayers for a sign had been answered! Emotion swept me like a gust of wind, and I almost cried uncontrollably. My eyes began to water, and my heart dropped in my chest. The rush of endorphins releasing within my body brought me a feeling of victory. Smiling abruptly, I buttoned up my uniform shirt with confidence. God heard my prayer for a sign—this I know for sure—and a speedy response it turned out to be! From that day forward, my uncertainty had been snuffed out with assurance from God himself. *God is in control*, I thought. I am thankful that the Lord allowed me to witness firsthand the glory of his hand when he gave me that sign to behold, because about two weeks later, my position as a firefighter/paramedic with this department would be no more.

Two weeks later around noon, we were taking count of the dive equipment on the dive apparatus when I received a tap on the shoulder. It was a fellow fireman notifying me that the training chief was on his way to talk with me. Once the training chief pulled up to the station and stepped out of his car, he waved me toward his SUV. He advised me that the fire chief (that is, the head chief) needed to see me. Concluding that this was doomsday for my career that had just begun, I exhaled and let the air conditioning graze along my skin, trying to allow myself to remain collected. In the conference room sat the head fire chief and his office assistant. Serving as a scribe for documentation, the office assistant was accompanied by her laptop, pecking at the keys in an effort to not miss a single word that was exchanged between the fire chief and me. "This department doesn't seem to be a good fit for you, Hogans. The crews feel as though you are not a team player." He continued, "We give all employees the option to resign as a courtesy, so the option is there for you. And Lorenzo, I want you to know that I do feel that you are a good firefighter and paramedic." There it was. The final words I would hear before signing the severance documentation. Of course the option to resign rather than to be terminated was the easy choice to make, and so I did. Once that ordeal was finished, a long, awkward ride back to the station with the training chief followed. My personal effects were still at the fire station and needed to be picked up, and I needed to clean out my locker. As I exited the station with my bags in hand, I firmly shook the hand of every member of the shift crew and told them how it had been a pleasure. The last person I bid a farewell to was the station captain who I thought had been an unreasonable person, yet I respected as a leader.

"The good news is that you start from scratch from this point onward," he said.

"Thanks for everything, and I think you are fine captain," I replied. Walking out of the exit door was an unusually and un-expectedly joyous moment. My thoughts were, "It's finally over; new beginnings are around the corner." I had not known at the time just what God had planned for my life next, but my confi-dence was heavily weighted on my faith that God would deliver me wherever he wanted me to be, just as he did with Moses as an infant.

Moses was placed in a river and sent away by faith. Miraculously, Moses was found by a member of the ruling family, making him royal. As I cruised home, I reflected on the events leading up to the present. Both relief and new confusion evolved from the silence I drove in. What would be my next move? How long would it be before my next job opportunity arose? Could I bounce back into the workforce in a timely fashion? Overloaded with thoughts firing from all directions, I diverted my mind else-where—my trust was in the Lord. For about an hour, I lay down in my bed before my girlfriend got back home. When she arrived, she curiously asked, "What are you doing home? Aren't you supposed to be working today?"

"It's over," I exclaimed. She was fully aware of the obstacles I had been faced with at my job, so she knew immediately what I was referring to. She broke down into a flood of tears as she pressed her cheeks on my chest. We embraced one another for a few moments as her tears soaked my T-shirt. "Everything will be okay," I told her. And I meant it: nothing was going to keep me back for long, at least if it was according to God's will, that is. Something you'll learn while trusting in God is that everything he allows or does not allow is an occurrence only made possible due to his greater plan for your life.

MISCHIEF

Only a few days had passed before I took it upon myself to get into some authentic mischief. To be a fireman, you have to be tobacco-free (and free from any other drugs) for a complete year prior to being hired. Most departments hold drug tests and conduct a polygraph test as an insurance policy for candidates. My mind had always been curious to know what the effects of marijuana felt like, so as you may imagine, my thoughts on the matter began to marinate, posing possibilities. I figured that with no job, there wasn't much to lose, and when else would I be able to experiment with "Mary J" without the paranoia of a random drug test being held above my head in the workforce? My girlfriend was no stranger to smoking pot, so she supplied the first blunt of the many subsequent blunts that would soon follow. "Here goes nothing," I thought to myself, inhaling the initial puff. Since this was my first time, getting high didn't take long.

My younger brother happened to be at my apartment that day hanging out with us. He enjoyed an occasional session of intoxication himself, experimenting with a hookah in addition to pot. My girlfriend prepared a hot plate of food fresh from the stove as I ascended higher and higher on cloud nine. I became fascinated with my brother's and girlfriend's facial expressions. My deep study of the two was hysterically interrupted by an outrageous intervention of obnoxious laughter. Any stare they gave me was only additional fuel for the comedy I had magically discovered. I felt like the Joker from *Batman*, unable to control my untamable humor, even though I attempted to muster up a serious demeanor and sit upright. My brother smirked, asking me something to the effect of, "Oh my gosh, what is wrong with you?" with a slight chuckle. Even this made me burst into tear-producing laughter. We turned on the television to listen to music, and my euphoria grew exponentially. I felt happy and hysterical about anything and everything. Not long after, I felt a rush of instant hunger deep within my stomach. My attention was stolen by the urge to consume a large quantity of food. My girlfriend must have known this, hence her cooking in the kitchen. She had delicious chicken, collards, macaroni, and mashed potatoes arranged on the plate so beautifully, it was as if the meal was a renowned work of art. Served alongside a tall glass of Gatorade, the pleasure was mine for the taking. And I took it, all right. Every bite was an explosion of memorable flavor, followed by exuberant splashes of flavorful liquid pouring down my throat. Soon after my meal, an overbearing haze came over me; it was time to lie down. Lying supine on the sofa, all I could do while in this state was hold on. I stared at the ceiling, waiting for a second wind that never came. All my chips had been cashed in, so to speak, and I was down for the count. When I woke up hours later, my girlfriend welcomed me back to earth. Hopeful to maintain the momentum, she offered to retrieve some mushrooms from her older brother so that we could "go on a trip." Feeling rebellious, I accepted the offer, figuring I ought to try it now while I didn't have a job to lose. The corridor of curiosity was wide open at this point in my life. The restrictions provided by the job I held were no longer in existence, so deeper into the experience I delved. At my girlfriend's older brother's house, we smoked marijuana, drank alcohol, and played cards. Four contenders gathered around a small table to partake in the game of spades. Once I was high again, my unstoppable laughter returned. Everyone was a comical genius when I was impaired. Spades carried on for a considerable amount of time, leading to the exchange of mushrooms from my girlfriend's older brother to her.

She drove us home to save us from getting into a vehicle accident. We laid the baggie of mushrooms on the kitchen counter, indulging in small talk regarding the alleged "trip" we were about to undergo. The consumption of the mushrooms left a unique taste in our mouths. This shouldn't have come to any surprise to us, for we were aware that the mushrooms were foraged out of cow manure. Again a sensation of humor overcame me, but this time things were different. I can vividly remember that humor did not reside in my system for long before a nostalgic effect came into play. I lay down to watch a movie with my girlfriend, falling into a deep state of reminiscence in my mind. My functionality minimal, I attempted to get up to use the restroom, but my body would not allow it. I wasn't able to fight the immobility, so I lay there, distracted by the colorful shapes and figures appearing intermittently. I had been watching a drug-induced slideshow of fragmented symbols that reminded me of my childhood. The colorful shapes and memorable toys that appeared in my hallucinations opened a window of past experiences, specifically all the way back to my preschool years. My girlfriend consoled me with a hand rubbing my back as I thought to myself, "I've lost control...And I don't like this...There are more productive things to be done than wallowing in my bed under the influence of recreational drugs." It was this particular thought that somehow gave me the willpower to stand up and walk to the bathroom. Kneeling down on one knee and planting one hand on the floor, I began to tear up. Sadness attacked me full force as I pondered why and how my life had come to what it was. As focused as I tried to be regarding the positive progression of my life and standards, I felt as though this very moment had to be rock bottom—the lowest of the low. "This was not in the plan," I thought. "How did I allow myself to fail?" I thought as loudly as if I had spoken the words.

I felt my girlfriend kneel down beside me. She asked me in a worried voice, "Is everything okay? What's wrong?" A ballistic tide of anger struck me that translated to silence. I gave no response, infuriated at the deterioration I allowed to come about. "Did everything just hit you all at once?" she asked.

"I'm fine," I finally responded in a calm tone. "Leave me to myself," I demanded, needing not consolation for my sorrows but isolation. Isolation to repair what was broken. Isolation to reflect on decisions I had made. Isolation to scold myself for the heap of rubble I had created. I was depressed and yet temperamental at the same time. The darkness encapsulated my mind like a door slowly shutting out any stream of light available. My candle had been snuffed, giving me a negative pulse of hopelessness. And then I remembered the sign that God had given me and began to pray from the depths of my heart. Something was missing. The grand puzzle in my mind seemed as though a piece was lost somewhere in the abyss. I remembered the scripture from the Bible that had to do with trials. David cries out to God in Psalms,

> O Lord my God, I take refuge in you; save and deliver me from all who pursue me, or they will tear me like a lion and rip me to pieces with no one to rescue me. O Lord my God, if I have done this and there is guilt on my hands—if I have done evil to him who is at peace with me or without cause have robbed my foe—then let my enemy pursue me and overtake me; let him trample my life to the ground and make me sleep in the dust. Arise, O Lord, in your anger; rise up against the rage of my enemies. Awake, my God; decree justice. Let the assembled peoples gather around you. Rule over them from on high; let the Lord judge the peoples. Judge me, O Lord, according to my righteousness, according to my integrity, O Most High. (Ps 7:1–8)

I was prepared for God's justice. I was prepared for God to do with me according to his will. The remembrance of scripture brought peace of mind. The belief that God had a plan was the firm position I decided to stand my ground with that night as I knelt down on my bathroom floor in despair.

A MEDICAL STORY

Red emergency lights and strobes flashed on the way to a call that dispatch had deemed a case of altered-level of consciousness. It was a beautifully bright day out as the ambulance skated along the roadways, careful not to turn over from bending around each corner. We approached the house we were responding to as we swerved through a middle-class subdivision like a serpent. In the rear of the establishment there lay a twenty-four-year-old male in a bedroom submerged in paraphernalia for marijuana. As we called to our patient in an urgent manner to wake up, the young man slowly rose to a seated position. His father had called 911 because prior to our arrival, he was unable to wake his son up, assuming then that he overdosed. Video game posters were falling off of his bedroom walls, dangling from the thumbtacks they were hanging from. The young man was blanketed in tattoos of fictitious video game characters such as the Super Mario Brothers.

I mention this medical story as an example of what debauchery can lead to. Debauchery can also be thought of as a vice or addiction. According to Dictionary.com, debauchery is the excessive overindulgence in sensual pleasures. Just as the night I immersed myself in recreational drugs, this man did so as well, except that he needed real attention from paramedics. When you bury yourself in the acts of debauchery, your self-control is compromised—even up to the point of life-threatening mishaps. God warns us for our own protection about losing ourselves and using those sensual pleasures: "Do not get drunk on wine, which leads to debauchery. Instead, be filled with the spirit" (Eph 5:18).

QUESTIONING PURPOSE

Losing my firefighter/paramedic job provoked me to question my purpose in life; not only my purpose but my passion as well. Maybe I had become a spoiled rotten egg over the years, but the fact is that I had grown so accustomed to things going as I planned them that having to resign from the fire department caught me like a blind man stuck in a tumultuous intersection. No preparatory measures had been put into place, for it was not my plan to *not* be working as a firefighter/paramedic. The first thing I needed to take care of was my financial well-being due to my girlfriend and her two-year-old son relying on me for support.

My father suggested that I apply for unemployment, which sounded ridiculous at first glance, because my assumption was that an individual could only be eligible if they were laid off, not if they resigned under duress, as my situation was. I had enough money in my bank account to survive off of for a little over a year thanks to my parents teaching me throughout my childhood the importance of saving. Depleting my life savings did not appeal to me, however, so I went with my parents' advice to file for unemployment. A few weeks later, the approval for my case was made! God blessed me with just the figure my monthly rent payment happened to be, too, as I was issued a one thousand dollar stipend per month for as long as four months. The stipulation was that I needed to submit five work applications per week to the unemployment agency. An additional blessing from God was at the fire department sent me a $1,800 retirement check owed to me from the city. I never dreamed I would be retiring by the age of twenty-four! Between the retirement check and the funds from the unemployment organization, a bit of time to collect myself became available to me. I now had four months to consider options and what direction I wanted to go. The daily regimen I concocted consisted of working out, swimming, reading, and going to church. Even the discovery of a new hobby came about by the name of Ultimate Frisbee. Every Sunday was a recreational field day filled with Ultimate Frisbee and a much older hobby of mine, soccer. Reading served as a form of meditation on what God might be calling me to do. I wanted to make sure that I could correctly identify what God's plan for me was because I believed that if I was in total sync with God's plan, success would be inevitable.

A MYSTERIOUS STRANGER

There's a story that ironically parallels this belief. It happened on June 22, 2014. It was a Sunday morning; I had just got out of morning church service. My parents enjoyed fellowshipping in the main social room where church staff placed complimentary coffee out, so my girlfriend and I met them in that pocket of the huge fellowship hall. Saying our goodbyes, my girlfriend and I proceeded to advance beyond the exit doors when I felt a finger tapping on my left shoulder. A middle-aged black gentleman looked at me with an expressionless face, saying, "There's someone that would like to see you." Flabbergasted, I walked with the man toward an older guy, also black, that stood about five feet, five inches tall and looked to be in his midsixties. His somber face intrigued me. "You're probably wondering why I asked you to come over here…The Lord has put a message in me to relay to you. I know you have seen a lot of things…and there's a lot that you have seen that you don't like," the older man said. "Things are about to get a lot better," he added. Who was this guy, and where did he come from? I asked myself.

"You don't believe me, do you? You probably think I'm crazy, don't you?" The old man asked. "The Lord told me that you are supposed to be a pastor," he added. He then turned to my girlfriend, looking immediately at me after he sized her up to possibly be my wife. "Is this your wife here?" He inquired.

"She's my girlfriend," I said.

"Well, if you like her, why don't you do like Beyoncé says and put a ring on it?" He playfully suggested. My girlfriend instantly grew fond of the man, applauding him for the strong suggestion by vigorously clapping her hands with a devious grin. Acutely returning to his grave nature, he leaned in and asked me, "You do know that if you're doing things the Lord's way, that he's obligated to help you, right?"

"Yes sir, I believe that," I replied. The serious yet playful gentleman gave us both a warm farewell, and we made our way to the exit doors for the second time. Astonished with what had just happened, the gears in my brain began to turn. Could this man have possibly been a prophet? It was certainly a possibility due to what the Bible tells us in 1 Corinthians 12. Listing nine different spiritual gifts through the spirit, the Bible indicates clearly,

> Now to each one the manifestations of the Spirit is given for the common good, to one there is given through the Spirit the message of *wisdom*, to another the *message of knowledge* by means of the same spirit, to another *faith* by the same spirit, to another gifts of *healing* by that one spirit, to another *miraculous powers*, to another *prophecy*, to another *distinguishing between spirits*, to another *speaking in different kinds of tongues*, and to still another the *interpretation of tongues*. All these are the work of one and the same Spirit, and he gives them to each one, just as he determines. (1 Cor 12:7–11, emphasis mine)

Further, there are many prophets in the Bible we read about carrying out God's will. Daniel was a prophet who interpreted mysterious dreams for King Nebuchadnezzar. Isaiah, Jeremiah, and Ezekiel were all major prophets. "But how does one determine the validity of an alleged God-inspired message by way of a prophet?" you might ask. The answer lies in Deuteronomy. "If what a prophet proclaims in the name of the Lord does not take place or come true, that is a message the Lord has not spoken. That prophet has spoken brazenly, so do not be alarmed" (Dt 18:22). His message seemed so interesting, although I did not put the chance of him being crazy past the reality of things.

FINDING PURPOSE

Finding purpose bombarded every corner of my mind, and I began reading books by Christians who wrote extensively on God's purpose for a person's life. King Solomon, one of the authors I studied, revealed it quite plainly to me in the last verse of Ecclesiastes. To keep God's commands was the overall purpose, according to scripture. Modern-day Christian authors advise the same thing in their books with proposals to hone the gifts that God blessed us with from birth, gifts meaning what you can do naturally better than most people. Putting it all together, faith had to be implemented in a life of purpose with God involved, and I understood that completely. There was no way of getting around the test of faith and the walk with God. My primary action was to seek the kingdom of God first, not worrying about tomorrow. "But seek first his kingdom and his righteousness, and all these things will be given to you as well. Therefore do not worry about tomorrow, for tomorrow will worry about itself. Each day has enough trouble of its own" (Mt 6:33–34). After about a month of collecting myself, I strapped on my two weight jackets that collectively weighed around seventy pounds. Living on the third floor spawned the idea to use the three-story staircase for endurance training. Hoping to regain what endurance I lost from not actively operating in the bunker gear I had grown accustomed to over almost a year with the fire department, I paced up and down my apartment's tall stairwell. Fortunately, my muscles in my legs felt pretty limber, signifying that progress was sure to be made in little time. I retested for my physical capabilities certification in order to apply for firefighting jobs again. The test tapped me for $140 total between the practical and video portions. The video portion evaluated human resource skills and functionality. For the following three to four weeks, I compiled a list of the departments I applied to. Arguments began to crescendo between my girlfriend and me during this phase. She wanted quality time with me that was beyond my mental desires, as I stared financial fears in the face. In the past I had gone through a brief period without a job, and it set me back almost all the way to zero dollars. My jar of coins was a last resort during that time to put a tank of gas in my car to appear for an interview at Family Dollar. Luckily, that job hired me because it had been the last bit of money I possessed at the time. Never wanting to face scarcity like that again, my head remained engrossed in finding income. Additional arguments evolved when my girlfriend decided to cease going to her part-time job while I was still unemployed. Everything was becoming a slow train wreck. My faithful 2003 Monte Carlo SS had even given me problems at this point, shutting off randomly every couple of drives. From mechanic to mechanic I jumped like a frog between lily pads to diagnose my car's issues. No one had a definitive answer outside of, "Your car seems to have a bad sensor." Though I replaced virtually every sensor under the hood, the problems persisted. The sums of money dished out to replace sensors began to add up. To make matters worse, my girlfriend's 2005 Dodge Neon locked up one day, needing a new set of brakes. Panic had not yet set in, as I continually hoped for the best, expecting things to change for the better in due time. Verbal sparring and hurtful degradation between my girlfriend and me grew more malicious. Verbal warfare transformed into domestic violence.

SHE LEAVES

On a gloomy morning, my girlfriend woke up beside me and told me that she was leaving. She felt that there was no reason to stay because major areas of life were not advancing, but rather halted in a state of limbo. Her words were, "Neither my family life, my financial state, nor my love life is flourishing, Lorenzo." It did not help that in an emotionally charged argument I told her to get out of my life in a fit of enraged anger. She also let me know that she felt like there was no purpose in staying since I yelled at her to give up. Her request was to be given fifty dollars before she left; she was going back to a deviant lifestyle that broke my heart—dancing. Oh, and not Broadway or ballet dancing either. The style of dancing she was going to return to required a minimal amount of clothing, if any at all. As she once before had done, she returned to stripping. Dishonored and dismayed, I did not hold her back from walking out, as much as it killed me on the inside to see her go. Deep down, the knowledge of her wanting to revisit such an ungodly profession trumped any irrational impulses to obstruct her that stemmed from my bleeding heart. Tears began to run down my cheeks when her son came to give me a goodbye hug before they left. I had grown attached to the little fellow. From frequent trips to the park to wrestling in the house, we spent a considerable amount of time together. He would copy certain ways he saw me do things like throwing a Frisbee or another saucer called an Aerobie disk. The little guy and I enjoyed many things, from the simplicity of taking a bath together to visiting big theme parks. "Bye, 'Renzo," he said to me in his high-pitched toddler voice. "Bye-bye," I responded, trying my hardest to keep the waterfall of tears from pouring out of my eyes uncontrollably.

CHAPTER 6

DEPRESSION

THE FRONT DOOR CLOSED BEHIND them, and I could only hold my composure long enough to get up and lock the door. Instantly, a violent storm of tears gushed from my eyes followed by a weakening pulsation that entered the top of my body and traveled down through my feet. My knees began to shake with weakness, soon making contact with the carpet, for I had fallen down in sorrow. For the first time in my life, I was all alone; the sense of abandonment struck me with brutal force, causing me to cry like a widow at the initial sight of her dead husband. Pain and agony overtook me; this by far was the most real emotion I had ever experienced. This event of lamentation left me in a state of utter ruin that day. Energy left my body faster than any fight, workout, or physical exertion had ever taken it from me. There was no trace of energy to be found in my cells. Appetite did not exist any longer in my body. All I could do was cry. When I was done crying, all I could do was cry some more. The world had turned its back on me, my girlfriend turned her back on me, and in that particular moment, it felt as though God himself turned his back on me.

After mourning for a period of time I cannot recall, I army-crawled from the kitchen tile to my sofa, using only my forearms to pull the rest of my body dragging across the floor—it was the best I could do. Pulling myself up on to the living room sofa, I then nestled myself closely in the posterior crevice of the couch to continue weeping until I fell fast asleep. When I woke up, still no appetite was present. Knowing that I had not eaten for upward of six hours, I forced myself to eat some oatmeal. Every scoop going down felt like a spoonful of clay going down my throat. Cotton mouth developed as if I was running an eight hundred meter race again—this had been the only occurrence in my past I had developed cotton mouth. Something had to give. Staying in such depression couldn't possibly be conducive to healthy living. Three things needed to be done. They were prayer, studying the scripture, and the rejuvenation of my physical and mental strength. Two days following my girlfriend bolting, I opened up my journal to begin a prayer log. Simultaneously, I opened up the Bible to the book of Psalms because I could remember verses on depression could be found there. To cover the third thing needed to be done, my workouts continued, though they were painfully forced. Knowing that interviews would be coming soon according to God's will, I had to be strong so I could perform well if required to do a physical test, as required by many fire departments in the interviewing process. Let me inform the reader that depression via genuine heartbreak is the single most devastating trial I have ever gone through.

I cannot imagine that it would be much different for anyone else. When you have sincerely invested yourself in a relationship that fails, darkness surrounds you as if someone has turned off the lights to the world. Subconsciously I had asked God what true emotion felt like on numerous accounts. There was a time when I questioned how normal I was because before undergoing the gut-wrenching blow of heartbreak, everything seemed trivial to me in regard to feeling emotional about something. Others seemed to experience true emotion while I remained detached. True loss occurs when you dare to love something more than yourself, and this was the monumental difference compared to any of my other endeavors. Vulnerability exposed me to such an occurrence as heartbreak. After all, I saw opportunity for love and attempted earnestly to seize it. And though the desperate battle I enrolled in to capture love was lost, regret did not fester inside of me whatsoever. When I saw opportunity, I reached for it, plain and simple. No regrets. Psalms brought me through the darkest hours of my life, and it will bring you through the darkest hours of your life. Depression had a strong hold on me like nothing you can fathom in your imagination. As I suffered from complete weakness, my uselessness converted into praise and worship.

SING

Remembering how King David as well as Paul would sing to the Lord in times of trouble, I decided to subscribe to this path. The psalm informs us, "The Lord is near to all who call on him, to all who call on him in truth. He fulfills the desires of those who fear him; he hears their cry and saves them" (Ps 145:18–19). Wanting to make sure God understood that I feared him, I let him know, exalting his very name while repenting of my sins before him through a river of tears. "The Lord is a refuge for the oppressed, a stronghold in times of trouble. Those who know your name will trust in you, for you, Lord have never forsaken those who seek you. Sing praises to the Lord, enthroned in Zion; proclaim among the nations what he has done. For he who avenges blood remembers; he does not ignore the cry of the afflicted" (Ps 9:9–12). These verses pierced my heart like an arrow. I took them to be my refuge, my saving grace. Elated to have some sort of action to take, I began to sing praises to God; this would symbolize my way of fighting this treacherous battle. Remembering hymns from an old church I once attended, the words began to flow from my mouth: "Lord prepare me to be a sanctuary...pure and holy...tried and true," I sang in the shower. While cooking I sang. At random parts of the day I would spontaneously break the silence in my apartment with singing praise to the Lord. Another song came to mind as I walked down my apartment's staircase one afternoon. The concluding song to church service every Sunday came to mind, and I would sing while walking, "The Lord bless you and keep you, the Lord make his face shine upon you. And give you peace, and give you peace, and give you peace forever." To the reader who may be depressed, understand that I feel your excruciating pain. I too have been there, and as your friend who loves you as a brother in Christ, believe me when I tell you that it gets better.

Two critical actions that can effectively transform depression into peace is active faith in the Lord through his Word and singing praise to God. It may feel funny at first, it may feel useless at first, but keep your head up and press on. During my depression, I felt as though the darkness was never going to end and I would never see the light of day again as long as I lived. Psalms helped me through these darkest of times, which were catalyzed by a broken heart. Confess your sins, lean on God, and hold on for deliverance. Above all, use these times of utter ruin to show God how unconditional your love is for him. Continue to thank him for how wonderful and gracious he is. When Paul and Silas were thrown into prison, they did not give in, turning their backs on the Lord who strengthened them. No, they sang hymns to God and stirred up an earthquake in doing so, allowing them to escape from confinement: "About midnight Paul and Silas were praying and singing hymns to God, and the other prisoners were listening to them. Suddenly there was such a violent earthquake that the foundations of the prison were shaken. At once all the prison doors flew open, and everyone's chains came loose" (Acts 16:25–26). Pay attention to the words of the last sentence: *Everyone's chains came loose.* I'm confident that your chains can come loose as well. Start singing, and start singing fast! God is waiting to hear the sound of your beautiful voice. It does not matter whether you sound like a broken record or not; God yearns to hear your pain and in turn will alleviate it.

SMALL TRIPS FOR EMPLOYMENT

Some of the seeds I planted started paying off, to my relief. Indian Rocks Fire Department called me for an interview. Interviews in the fire department typically have processes that encompass about four or five steps: first, the submission of your application. Second, a panel interview. A panel interview consists of anywhere from three to seven interviewers. If you're invited back to interview again, it usually is a one-on-one style interview with the head chief. If you do well with the head chief's interview, a polygraph test still has to be passed to reveal whether or not you have been truthful about everything on your application—most importantly the questions about drug use. This interview that I was granted happened to be the panel interview. When I walked into the conference room, six men greeted me with firm handshakes. It lasted about twenty minutes, and I concluded that things went very well—I was wrong. The letter in the mail from them read, more or less, "Thanks for trying." This was a small failure, but the likelihood of receiving more interviews due to my applying to twenty-five locations—coupled with faithful prayer in my journaling log—kept me hopeful. Next I would travel about two hours away from my hometown, Saint Petersburg, Florida, to Kissimmee. Their hiring evaluation included an advanced life support test (practical) and fire grounds test. My feelings were that I aced the medical scenario they tested me on, yet I could have done better on the fire grounds portion of the assessment. Ocala would be my next interview, which also included a physical fire grounds portion as well as a panel interview.

WORST PERFORMANCE EVER

Being a competitor, this performance assessment almost took the wind from my sails; this day was without a doubt the most horrific physical performance of my life! I hydrated myself sufficiently the night prior and leading all the way up to test time. However, the lifeless spaghetti-like nature my entire body resembled when I exerted myself did not reflect any kind of preparation. Blazing rays of the sun baked my body underneath the already hot conditions of wearing bunker gear. Advancing a hose lay, setting up a ladder, performing a blindfolded search, and carrying a 175-pound mannequin one hundred feet were all tasks that I needed to perform. About halfway through testing, my body overheating and almost entirely drained, I bargained with my conscience to quit. The portion of the physical assessment when this occurred was a segment where I had to use a ten-pound sledgehammer to move a metal sled about three feet. Expending every morsel of energy within me, I had bent over with an episode of lightheadedness like none other. Thanks to the mixture of the dizziness, heat, energy scarcity, and a mouth that was drier than the Sahara Desert, I argued with myself between the options of quitting versus continuing forward. Quitting was not in my nature, so telling myself that today would not be the start, I struggled to lift the sledgehammer subsequently to move the metal slab three feet. By the time this station was finished, I felt like death on a platter. Completing this feat brought me to the final segment—carrying the 175-pound mannequin backward one hundred feet to the finish line. Deep, methodical breaths entered and exited my lungs as I closed my eyes for an attempted miniature meditation before my final hoorah. Squatting down behind the deadweight mannequin, I thrust my legs up with all of my might to elevate the dummy off of the ground so I could start walking backward. Halfway to the finish line, my desperate desire was to drop the dummy on the ground, take a breather, and then continue. The only problem with that idea was that I didn't believe that there was enough power within me to pick the mannequin back up! "Keep walking," I motivated myself under dire conditions. Finally, in my periphery, I could see cones—the finish line cones, that is. My nightmare was over; I could die now in that instant having not quit. Water was the only thing on my mind; I was longing for cold, thirst-quenching liquid to splash every taste bud I had. Someone thankfully brought out a large cup of water so that I could replenish at least some of the fluids my pores had lost through excessive diaphoresis. There was no question about whether my chances were good enough to be offered employment with Ocala; failure was evident on every bit of that performance. I didn't even get an opportunity to dry off before the panel interview portion of the department's evaluation took place. Sitting comfortably in the cool, air-conditioned room, my arms drenched the seat they gave me, and it was obvious. I knew that the men on the panel were merely going through the motions at this point because they had all been outside to witness firsthand the atrocity I disgraced myself with in the pitiful performance. They kept things professional and cordial, which inwardly I appreciated.

The ride back home was one of grave disappointment. Normally my music was playing, but no, not this time. Basking in shame seemed to be what I needed. Beyond that, my mind was obsessively set upon making sense of what just happened. This was the first time I seriously considered quitting. Winning is a part of having a competitive spirit, but no excuse could possibly be derived in order to explain the shameful loss I had just incurred. The sad, desolate drive home turned into a sad, desolate day altogether. I was licking my wounds the entire day and night. I needed to overturn this loss with a win to forget about the current pain I felt. Documenting this experience as I documented everything in my prayer journal, I closed my notebook at night, marking the cessation of my sulking.

NEW OPPORTUNITIES

Just four hours after the deadline to apply to Oviedo Fire Department, the phone rang with the voice of the administrative assistant extending an invitation to me to interview. This was the rebound to spring back into action with a win! Interviewing with Oviedo proved to be phenomenal. God blessed me with a great overall interview. I answered every question they asked as if I already knew the line of questions. Head nods and smiles filled the conference room we sat in. Just hours after I left the interview, Oviedo Fire Department called me back to schedule a polygraph test. Already having interviewed with another agency in Manatee County, I now had two places that I longed to hear from. A conditional offer was made from the Manatee County agency, and just in time might I add. God's timing was superb, for my unemployment benefits would expire within a week outside of my start date at my new job! Giving thanks and praise to the Lord, I began to see the Lord's faithfulness to me in an authentic form. It didn't stop there, however. Looking back on my prayer journal, keeping a ledger proved to be more useful than simply recording prayers; it was a form of documentation of events that occurred. Ironically, I found that the day after the worst performance of my life took place in Ocala was when the County of Manatee made me a conditional offer of employment!

CHAPTER 7

RENEWAL

IT AMAZED ME THAT I had not realized that God awarded me a job back directly after being in the dumps about the failure I incurred upon myself the day prior! What I learned from this blessing was that it's never pointless to keep faith in the Lord, because we do not know his plans. Though the worst physical performance of my life added to the depression and darkness that submerged me, out of the darkness came light! Trust in the Lord with all your heart; he has plans for you.

MEN'S BIBLE STUDY STORY

Thursday nights at my church were the designated nights for men's Bible study. There I met a nice man on the first day who issued the program binders filled with material. A one-year Bible reading plan, a Bible, and worksheets were a few things in this binder. As we sat down in a circle, this nice man explained to us how we would see God's plan unfold before our eyes. He told of how when he initially joined the church, he was a construction

man, primarily building Walmart stores. The mind-boggling irony of it all is that for years God had him working on the construction of Walmarts, and our church had been a Walmart prior to
being a church. When they called a team together to renovate
the old Walmart building into a church establishment, you'll
never guess who was on that team. That's right, this gentleman,
who much of his career practiced for God's construction team!

Now is the time to submit to faith in God. God has a pan-
oramic view of all that has gone on, goes on, and will go on
in your future. Faith can be more important and effective than
understanding in terms of the Lord's plans. It's a basic want to
crave understanding, but the reality of it is this: understanding
something doesn't always mean you can change its outcome, especially when it's concerning God's will!

NEWNESS

The timing couldn't have been better. Understanding that my
vehicle did not have much time left until its inoperable end,
searching for a new automobile moved into the highest slot
of priorities on my list. The trade-in value of my car stood at
$3,000. No private party was going to buy a car that intermit-
tently shuts off, so I didn't bother wasting time trying to sell to
an uninterested audience. Done with spending money on repair
attempts, the only option left was to purchase a car and get as
much as the dealership would offer for my automobile as a trade-
in. Upfront I told them how problematic my 2003 Monte Carlo
SS had become so they did not feel as if I was trying to pull any
punches. My hopes were to get the maximum advertised trade-in
value for the horrible condition my vehicle was in. As far as I'm
concerned, there's nothing wrong with wishful thinking. With

my fingers crossed, dealerships and online automobile vendors were my focus for a couple of weeks. Intense searches and inquiries were carried out; my new job did not need its newest employee breaking down constantly on his way to work. I prayed for grace in finding the right car to suit my list of "must haves." Fuel economy, the year, size, shape, and color all contributed to my conceptualized selection I had predetermined. As I filed through vehicle after vehicle online, there it was. The second my "would be" car appeared on the computer screen, my fingers had already begun excitedly dialing the dealerships contact number for sales. "Hold the pearl Malibu with two-toned leather," I happily told the sales manager over the phone. "I'll be there in no more than two hours." Test-driving it gave me goose bumps as I cruised down the freeway; my new car and I were a perfect match. It also pleased me to have found one with all of the options I had written down on my preconceived wish list. Sunroof, leather seats, power seats, remote start, low mileage: everything was there. Getting back from the test drive marked the start of a monotonous four-hour wait in the lobby.

Thankfully, I had nowhere to go at a scheduled time, because those plans would have been ruined. If anyone would have told me it took that long to finalize buying a car, I wouldn't have believed it. But then again, this was the first time ever purchasing a car from a dealership. Appraisal of my old vehicle's trade-in value matched the online quote I had hoped and prayed for. God blessed me favorably with the ability to apply my old car toward the purchasing price of my new car via trade-in. Things were starting to come together. A gentleman at my federal credit union assisted me with an auto loan with low monthly payments. Business at the federal credit union ran smoothly, as smooth as I could ask for. Not only had it been my first time purchasing a car from a dealership, but it was also my first time pursuing an auto loan. Momentum in a positive direction accumulated thanks to God's blessings on my life. 2014 had been the most devastating year in all of my life. My career, my romantic relationship, and my car added up to be the three most important things that I personally cherished, and now two out of the three of these losses had been returned as if they had only been temporarily borrowed. My faith in the Lord blossomed as time progressed. Not many instances do you hear about an individual buying a car while unemployed. Well, to be technical, there were only two more weeks before my start date when I purchased the new automobile. Savings lessons from my parents paid off over the years because then the usefulness of having a nest egg for unexpected expenses became exceedingly evident.

Orientation at my new emergency medical systems job as a paramedic was a bore. Normally the agency held a two-week orientation with eight-hour training days. Because my hiring class happened to be hired during the holidays, the training division decided to cut orientation for us down to a week and a half, ten-hour days apiece. Training lieutenants took turns coming in and out of the main workshop room to lecture. Just about every one of them had a cup of coffee in their hands while teaching the tedious information, giving the new recruits the impression that the training staff was struggling to stay awake just as much as we were! Each morning on the way to work, I prayed for strength to bear the turbulence my mind was in. Being all alone was a challenge for me, considering I was used to having my girlfriend to communicate with as my aid. Aside from that, I had been alone in an unfamiliar territory. Traveling to a new county gave me an indescribable feeling. I didn't know whether to be happy for new beginnings or sad. There weren't any hometown friends to call on. "A fish out of water" is how the saying goes, and this suddenly meant more to me now that I was experiencing it. Jesus was with me through these times of discomfort. A sense of displacement caused me to rely on what I knew gave me a sense of home, my friend Jesus Christ. I found myself getting unusually close with Jesus throughout each day. Something tells me that Jesus didn't mind either, because when comfort levels are high and your plans are being carried out according to plan, we tend to turn up life's volume, drowning out the voice of Christ in our lives. Too many times we are sidetracked with personal interests, pleasures, and all-around nonsense—as if these things hold any value at all when compared with Christ.

As sure as the grass is green, I can vouch for God when I tell you that he is good. God was my refuge during unfamiliar, uncomfortable times such as these. Talking with God soothed my doubts upon letting him know all of my troubles. A vital part of relying on Jesus as a refuge was undoubtedly keeping the belief that his plans were sound. I'm convinced that some people get confused into thinking that once you pray, all you have to do is sit around and wait for an angel to come knocking on your door. My advice is to get active and stay active. The Bible does tell us that if you ask you shall receive, but it's not like you just ask for the winning lottery ticket and it's magically mailed to you. Avoid distorting scripture as some prosperity teachers tend to do. We have the spiritual responsibility to give God something to bless, and that includes more than a mere prayerful request. God wants to see his people in action. Be active, *not* reactive. "For the Spirit God gave us does not make us timid, but gives us power, love and self-discipline" (2 Tm 1:7).

MOVING

The lease date on my apartment grew nearer and nearer until the time came to move out. I called my good friends up to help move all my belongings down from my third-floor apartment into a U-Haul truck. My good friends Jarred, Errol, Chris and my nephew Cyrus were reliable when needed. It was a job made exponentially less difficult with four extra pairs of hands to help move furniture and the like. True allies are tough to come by; don't ever forsake those that prove to be loyal to you. From about 7:00 a.m. to noon we worked, packing the U-Haul and transporting the load to my sister's garage, where it would all sit for a fifteen-day layover. Since my new apartment's move-in date created a fifteen-day gap from my old apartment, I would have to stay at my father's house in his guest bedroom, which was my old bedroom. I'm thankful for having the support I've been blessed with, especially during instances such as this. Dragon Ball Z magazines, Pokémon cards, comic books, old trophies, and pictures of my favorite Redskins running back, Clinton Portis, were still in my old closet; they induced nostalgia as I examined each of them. In the hall closet, which held family games, sat what my father and I would compete in for the next few days—chess. Having learned at a very young age from my father, I was anxious to try my hand at beating him. Three times we played one another, jockeying for position with our pawns and jousting with our knights. I won all three games, but it wouldn't be long before we migrated to an area of competition my dad was more seasoned in than I was. Since my father retired, he spent most of his recreational time toward the development of his golf game. The driving range seemed to be his second home by the way he smacked the golf ball out into the distance. It took precious time for me to even make good contact, let alone drive the ball into the abyss like he did.

We teed off on the putting green in an intense precision putt. This particular area of golf proved to be my strength. Whether the putt was short or long, accuracy was evident in my strokes, and I made sure my dad heard a good amount of trash talk since I couldn't do so on the driving range due to my subpar swings.

While still in town, I made sure I took my nephew to the basketball courts to play pickup. We loved two-on-two challenges on the court. He had an unforgettable three-point shot, and mine wasn't bad either. We both had speed too, making us a difficult duo to manage. My mother told me how school was going for her; she worked on her Bible classes diligently most nights of the period I spent there. Mom always kept a Bible verse in her back pocket. If you were to open her Bible, you'd see a rainbow of colors throughout the pages. These colors were the highlighters she would use to save her favorite scripture verses. Much of my faith is credited to my mother; I think of it as a ricochet of her relentless poise in the Word.

CHAPTER 8

SIGN NUMBER TWO

ROUGHLY THREE YEARS SPANNED THE investment of energy and effort toward my relationship with my ex-girlfriend, making moving on a hard pill to swallow. Daily reminiscing on memories we
shared taxed my mind. Living together was a fatal mistake since
our cohabitation occurred premaritally. Being sexually intimate
before marriage turned out to be a big mistake too. People rave
about defiling themselves, whether it be through sexual immorality, drunkenness, or greed; what people don't boast about is
the hangover. I realize that God actually counsels us for good
reason, not because he doesn't want to see his children happy.
The truth is, we generally think we can outsmart the system
when it comes to getting away with whatever we want to do in
opposition with God's will. We make excuses. We rationalize. We
twist up the Word of God to squeeze our own selfish desires into
the frame, reasoning that somehow we are the exception. There
is our way, and then there's God's way. Our way inevitably sets
us back on scheduled blessings. Waiting isn't by any means the
ideal way to obtain what we want, but when we're waiting on God

to give the go-ahead, we must exercise discipline to heed self-control long enough for God's plan to unwind. The alternative is to learn the hard way, and let me tell you, it truly is the hard way in every sense of the word when we choose our own way.

Like most of you, I longed for love via a romantic relationship, and sinful desires such as premarital sex were included. I set out to find it back in 2011, surfing through Facebook pages to find a candidate. It didn't take long to find a young, beautiful woman to match my wants. She seemed to want the same romantic love that I desired, so we hit it off in no time flat. She was a New Yorker with a set of brown eyes that could leave you frozen in time. Her hair flowed elegantly down her back. Her olive skin grew a more brilliant color from the tan only a hot Florida sun could grant. I love women from New York because they can always talk for days about nothing much at all, and with optimal enthusiasm. Approximately three months into our relationship, she called me over to her house to share some life-altering news—she was pregnant. She was three and a half months pregnant from her previous boyfriend; therefore a decision had to be made. Either I was in or I was out. Most guys would run for cover upon hearing this sort of news, but not me, not this time. I considered my options and convinced myself that it wouldn't be terrible—this ought to give you a ballpark idea of how much I longed for love and also how much I liked this woman. My thought process in the situation was that if I chose to stay with her, I would have gained a loyal soul mate for life. She fit everything I wanted in a female—for the most part anyway. I vowed to continue forward with her through the thick and the thin, and we proceeded in our romance. Little did I know that my theory of staying in the relationship had many holes; things got tough for her after the pregnancy, and she turned to stripping for the first time.

Disgusted, I let her know that there was no place for that foolishness with me. We parted ways for about eight months. My current job working part-time at the local grocery store was not enough to support her and her child, and my eyes were set on graduating from paramedic school. Eight months later, my graduation came along with her breaking up with the guy she had been dating. Shortly after graduation, God blessed me with my firefighting/paramedic job at the local fire department. Agreeing that she would turn away from the promiscuous dancing, we gave our relationship a second try. Things started out perfect this time around; she agreed that she would pick up a part-time job that was respectable, and my full-time status at the fire department alone could take care of all the bills. I moved her and her son into my apartment. Between camping trips, family visits out of town, going to theme parks, and other adventures, love was in the air. Hate was in the air as well, for we bumped heads quite a bit on multiple issues. Nonetheless, we kept the ball rolling, accepting the highs and lows of being together, charging it to the name of love. She was hands down and hats off the toughest woman I had ever known. She possessed the beauty of a queen yet the ruggedness of a tomboy. I enjoyed outdoor activities very much, and so did she, making recreational activities limitless with her. She wasn't afraid to sweat or get dirty. As radiant as she was, working out and playing outdoor sports was not beneath her; in fact she loved it. True friendship is what we shared, like none other I had ever experienced from a female. I guess that's why heartbreak consumed me so following severance from her. One night as we lay next to one another, we discussed secrets that we might not have shared with each other yet. We wanted to clear the air about any possible deal breakers on the relationship.

And then it hit me like a semitruck going a hundred miles per hour: "Lorenzo, I have an STD."

What could it possibly be? I thought to myself in the pitch-black darkness. Nearly sweating, I slowly opened my mouth and asked, "Do you have HIV or AIDS?"

"No," she replied. I thought to myself, thank God.

"I have herpes, Lorenzo," she said from the cold darkness. Anger filled my veins, making my blood boil beyond a fathomable temperature. Inclined to turn over and choke the life out of her, I calmly rekindled my sanity. It had been over two years of knowing her at this point, and the betrayal I felt cannot be described. How could someone do this? How could someone be so inhumane? How could a person be so selfish? Two things were considered that night as I lay in the bedroom in complete discombobulation. My first inclination was to strangle her to death, as I already mentioned. The second option was to forgive her. Weighing in the fact that I probably had herpes myself from the occasional unprotected sex we had made me feel that it was pointless to do anything out of anger. That night I decided to stick it out with her because for one, I figured I acquired the disease, and for two, I still loved her.

As you already know, things didn't work out for the second time once I lost my job. She turned to dancing again once a slew of arguments and domestic violence occurrences left our relationship in ruins. During the time of my being down in the dumps, however, God both blessed me and awarded me a sign. The blessing came in the form of test results. Just a few days after my ex-girlfriend stormed out of my apartment, my first concern was to get tested for herpes. Among the clinics that performed STD testing, I chose the clinic with the shortest turnaround time for results. Only twenty-four hours did I wait to receive my negative result: I did not acquire herpes. Relief came over me, and I praised God for his mighty grace.

Also, a revelation came to me in the midst of my depression. Crying out to God, I begged him to show me a sign that he was listening to me. I requested counsel from God mainly for dealing with my loss of companionship. On Monday, November 10, 2014, I sent this prayer up to the Lord, asking that he respond to me in a dream. That very night, God fulfilled my request in my dreams. There sat a man on a bench who spoke to me with such grace, but whose face I cannot recall. He told me that my longtime romantic companion was *presumptuous* and *impotent*. Immediately waking up to a gasp of fresh air, I sat up to write down the words on a sheet of paper. Around 3:00 a.m. is when this occurred. My body exhausted, I fell back into a peaceful slumber. How do I know that this dream came from God? There are two reasons, at least. First, I will have the reader know that I did not know the definitions to these words prior to looking them both up as soon as I awoke! It's not as if I knew these words' implications or definitions. Second, the words' definitions describe my ex-girlfriend's actions to a tee. According to an online dictionary, the definition of *presumptuous* is "failing to observe the limits of what is permitted or appropriate." A synonym for presumptuous is *brazen*, which is defined as "shameless." This points to the act of stripping, a decision she chose to toil in twice. The other vocabulary word, *impotent*, is defined as "unable to take effective action; helpless or powerless." A synonym for *impotent* is *futile*, which means "incapable of producing any useful result; worthless." Reading these definitions brought me to tears. I cried out to God, asking him to help me manage the pain. How clear of a message he had given me! And not to mention, it was not a rosy one!

From me to you, understand that these words given to me in my dream were not hallucinated or concocted in my own brain out of hatred for my ex-girlfriend. Though deeply hurt by our cessation of companionship, love is still and always will be in my heart for her, no matter what. Like you may be wondering, I wondered why God would send me a message exclaiming that *anyone* was shameful and worthless, especially someone that I love so dearly. My heart froze over upon reading the peculiar message I received. Deciding to look further into the divine dream I'd experienced, opening my Bible was my first action for additional clarity. As blatant as the dream's message was, accepting these powerful words at face value did not sit well in my conscience, though I did accept it. To the outsider looking in, a message such as this may seem trivial with no emotional attachment. But when I tell you that I struggled desperately with the loss of the woman I considered marrying, nothing could compare to the heartbreak deep within the inner parts of my soul. Pondering what God meant about her being worthless left me in an odd position. Imagine loving someone, only to hear from God that they are worthless. The verse that gave me great clarity on the matter came from 1 Samuel: "Eli's sons were worthless men. They had no regard for the Lord" (1 Sm 2:12). My ex-girlfriend attended church regularly, we prayed together, and we even made sure that she recited the prayer of repentance. Unfortunately there was one thing that she stubbornly refused to repent for; she felt no need to. Our second run at dating one another spawned much-needed areas for discussion. I came to her, sincerely stressing the need of repentance for her acts of degrading herself as a stripper. She bumptiously maintained her personal view of nothing at all being wrong with the dancing. When we choose to hold no regard for the Lord, we fall into the category of being worthless.

Another symptom of having no regard for the Lord's commands is called hardening your heart toward God. I'm guilty of this offense. You're guilty of this offense. We all have been guilty of this offense. Intentionally being nonchalant toward the Holy Word, turning our heads away from divine direction, and inadvertently choosing to act against the wisdom God instills puts us on the fast track to becoming worthless in the eyes of the Lord Almighty. Holding God's commands in contempt is like building a brick wall, obstructing our usefulness to God. Hardening your heart is indeed a choice. Only one recorded person's heart was hardened by God himself. "But the Lord hardened Pharaoh's heart and he would not listen to Moses and Aaron, just as the Lord had said to Moses" (Ex 9:12). God hardened Pharaoh's heart for his divine purposes; we know this by scripture saying so in Romans: "For Scripture says to Pharaoh: I raised you up for this very purpose, that I might display my power in you and that my name might be proclaimed in all the earth" (Rm 9:17). There is no sense in jeopardizing the fulfillment of your true purpose, so avoid hardening your heart at all costs. God put you here to live as Christ did. An optimal example to model, living like Christ did, gives onlookers a true observation of servant leadership. Not leading by example negatively alters the amount of nonbelievers willing to accept Christ into their lives. Peace, joy, love, and happiness are attractive characteristics to model. Others that observe these types of traits will both appreciate and seek these traits for themselves: "To open their eyes and turn them from darkness to light, and from the power of Satan to God, so that they may receive forgiveness of sins and a place among those who are sanctified by faith in me" (Acts 26:18). Sin is in our inner dwellings. Sin lives down inside of us so far that it cannot be captured, bagged up, and tossed into a trash can. For this subtle reason, we can thankfully turn to repentance.

Pay close attention to the sins you love most; it is these particular angles Satan delights to ambush you with. Take my life, for example: sexual immorality, an abomination to God, infiltrated my life and mind because I had not been firm in my walk with the Lord. Sex is made for the marriage bed for many wonderful reasons, all of which to serve as protection for God's children. Think about STDs. Think about having children under unintentional circumstances. Think about the pain felt when you give yourself to someone, become attached, and then have to say goodbye. When you have sex with a person, a chemical is released called *oxytocin*, often referred to as the "cuddle drug." More potently released in women, this natural hormone induces feelings of attachment. All sorts of endorphins are released as well, cumulatively creating a unique bond between two persons. We don't think about all of the fine print when signing up for pleasure, and in turn we suffer the repercussions. King David had issues in this department. King Solomon above all had problems in this department. Samson lost his God-given supernatural strength due to issues in this department of sin. King Herod had John the Baptist beheaded because Herod was pleased by a dance. Some dance this must have been—Herod even gave an oath to relinquish up to half of his kingdom! King Herod also stole his wife, Herodias, from his brother, Philip. King Ahab was manipulated and pushed as a victim to this vice. I myself was a hair away from getting herpes to have and to hold for the rest of my life. How nice would that have been? Explaining that I have an incurable disease to every person I dated? The corridor of sin I speak to you so candidly about at this moment cannot be taken lightly; the cost is too high. The Bible speaks strongly against sin, but notice the verbiage the Lord gives in regard to sexual immorality. The Bible uses a unique word that is defined as "a thing that causes disgust or hatred." The word I speak of used by the Lord is *abomination*. 1 Corinthians says, "Flee from sexual immorality. Every other sin a person commits is outside the body, but the sexual immoral person sins against his own body. Or do you not know that your body is a temple of the Holy Spirit within you, whom you have from God? You are not your own, for you were bought with a price. So glorify God in your body" (1 Cor 6:18–20).

CHAPTER 9

BEING SINGLE

ALWAYS HAVING A COMPANION HAS a tendency to create codependen-cy. As an affectionate, loving person, one of my things was to always have some type of romance going on in my life. Further, the desire for companionship developed into a must-have men-tality for me. Half of the time I would date women that I didn't even like. As social media continues to reinforce what we must have to bring happiness, it is true that our own voices are not the only voices pressuring and suggesting what is good in our minds. For the life of me, I couldn't figure out why the relationships I kept failed so frequently. If you find yourself in a similar pre-dicament as I was in once, consider a few things scripture taught me. Being single is a good thing. Depression forced me to learn that it's perfectly okay to be single. Fears of loneliness, feelings of inadequacy, and feelings of worthlessness are all leading fears that are much smaller dilemmas than we often make them out to be. I realized that the primary reasons that my relationships fail constantly is because my companion did not hold the same set of values I did, or I didn't like them to begin with. That's right—sometimes I dated girls that truly I didn't have much interest in at all. In fact, I did this number quite a bit. This is the sad result of codependency. The feeling that you can't manage without being in a relationship with someone yields many weaknesses. This fallacy breeds unattractive character traits as well. Be your own person. If you're only ever known as an individual who's one half of an irrelevant pair, your true value will have a lot harder time shining through. Paul said that he wished everyone could be single like him. We're talking about arguably the greatest Christian that ever lived! "I wish all of you were as I am. But each of you has your own gift from God; one has this gift, another one has that. Now to the unmarried and widows I say: it is good for them to stay unmarried, as I do. But if they cannot control themselves, they should marry, for it is better to marry than to burn with passion" (1 Cor 7:7–9). Paul speaks of how it is better to be single because he was pleased with how much he was able to accomplish as a single male. Being single is essentially less of a burden if you can handle it, according to Paul. The hierarchy of responsibility for a married man is the needs of God, the wife, children if kids are in a man's life, and then the man himself. Without a wife, there is no female to be held responsible for because the second line of duty for a married man is to take care of his spouse. Paul stresses how he was not tied down to this particular responsibility, enabling him to solely focus on pleasing the Lord. Steer clear of entertaining people that you can clearly see are going to be temporarily in your life. What sense does it make to extend your time and energy on a flop? More importantly, how much sense does it make to become emotionally invested in a nonbeliever? The answer is none at all.

A great book to refer to for wisdom on finding a worthy mate is the book of Proverbs. Your time is precious; don't waste it on irrelevant relationships as I did for many years as a result of being codependent. Some obvious deal breakers for individuals that won't be right for an upstanding Christian man or woman are ungodly traits such as selfishness, greed, lying, arrogance, etc. Proverbs spells out what is permissible in a companion. Better to be single than to be taken by a person you clearly are not compatible with. An absolute, no-questions-asked standard for a believer is to date another believer. Being equally yoked irrefutably accounts for the retention statistics in Christian marriages. Christian marriages are the leading category of stability in marriage according to a book called *The Good News about Marriage*.

INTERACTION WITH A PATIENT

Every now and again I get the pleasure of chatting with outgoing patients on the ride to the hospital. One patient's name was Donald; he was sixty-six years of age. As I asked him questions regarding his medical history, prescribed medications, allergies, etc., he playfully informed me that he faithfully takes Viagra. Chuckling at his comment, I replied, "You gotta do what you gotta do," as I recorded his personal information.

He sighed before he said, "Then again, the wife is pretty much to the point where she could care less if we did the deed or not."

"How long have the two of you been married?" I inquired.

Donald replied, "Forty-six years...Yep, she's a good one, the only woman I've ever been married to."

"Forty-six years is quite some time to be married, sir; what's the secret to long-lasting marriage? Nowadays, the overall marriage divorce rate is about fifty percent," I exclaimed.

Donald readjusted himself on the stretcher before revealing, "My wife and I are both Christians; that is what created such longevity. Any time difficulties arise, we both put our faith in Jesus Christ, and we are strengthened," Donald announced. He asked me if I was a Christian, and I told him I had been a believer for quite a while. If you look at the marriage statistics, they point to values and standards held in partners, which is why Christians have the longest retention rates in marriage. When dating potential candidates for marriage, keep in mind that both the Bible and statistics show the secret to a lasting marriage.

One service I attended gave me encouragement from a gentleman by the name of Frank who caught up with me directly after the closing prayer. I shared my story of returning to the Lord, which included the loss of my romantic relationship, at a men's Bible study. Frank confidently expressed to me through a story of his own that God would restore my romantic life when he was ready. Frank exclaimed to me that he wrote a letter to God when he was single. He delightedly said, "I placed my letter on the dresser and just left it there. I didn't bother mentioning it to God again; I simply placed my letter of request on my bedroom dresser and waited. Six months passed, and there she was," Frank said, pointing to his wife. "We've been married for six years now," he said with a huge smile on his face. Marriage is a lifelong commitment that many desire for their lives.

Now I will share a few things the Bible advises about finding a marriage partner: "Do not be yoked with unbelievers. For what do righteousness and wickedness have in common? Or what fellowship can light have with darkness? What harmony is there between Christ and Belial? Or what does a believer have in common with an unbeliever?" (2 Cor 6:14–15). Marriage retention statistics prove this instruction to be accurate. Believers belong with believers. Take my story of Donald as a prime example. His confidence in the length of his marriage was completely placed in the Bible's instruction! Forty-six years is not a short marriage! Just as the scripture suggests, what do a believer and a nonbeliever have in common? For those of you who are believers that have tried to be yoked with a nonbeliever, it is clear that there are vast differences between the two. Decisions are based off of beliefs an individual holds. In order for a couple to be in sync when it comes to decision making, the two companions must first hold the same beliefs and values. If your desired mate does not believe in the Bible, his or her actions and decisions will reflect this. This takes a toll on the believer and nonbeliever alike, making for an unnecessarily stressful relationship. Trust me by the testimonies and personal experiences I share to avoid such dealings with nonbelievers as marriage contenders. Ensure that both you and your partner are saved to avoid the disappointment, the heartbreak, and the truthful statistics that say secular marriages just don't tend to last. The Bible encourages life compatibility in terms of life purpose in the book of Amos: "Do two walk together unless they have agreed to do so?" (Am 3:3). Marriage is a spiritual contract that says two people walk in agreement. Life purpose is such a critical subject to cover when selecting a mate so that the walk together is smoother. If the parties do not know their life purposes, then there is no need to force a square peg through a round hole. Trying to select a life partner prior to having identified your life purpose will create a confusing relationship. The result of doing this produces directionless conversations, motives, and desires that in turn reflect a lack of ambition.

Blowing like a leaf in the wind is the same as not having your life purpose. Without purpose there is no concrete direction. With no concrete direction, you will not even recognize negative setbacks for what they are. When you lack concrete direction, life tends to make you lackadaisical and reactive to circumstances. What's worse than one person reacting to life circumstances is *two* people merely reacting to life circumstances in unison. I once asked a woman I dated what she thought her life's purpose was; she told me that she felt her purpose was to be there for herself and her family. These both are noble things to do, yet they lack true purpose. I asked another girl I dated what she thought the meaning for existence was, and she candidly claimed that her purpose was to take care of her son, live a decent life, and eventually become food for the worms when she hit the dirt. You can see the extremely overt responses that nonbelievers can have. Another person I asked the purpose for his existence responded with: "To live well, leave a mark, and die." He also felt that once he died, there was no heaven or hell waiting on him.

The Bible instructs us to not be associated with those that have uncontrollable tempers. "Do not make friends with a hot tempered person, do not associate with one easily angered, or you may learn their ways and get yourself ensnared" (Prv 22:25). Uncontrollable anger reveals low self-worth. Emotional health factors carry great weight in relationships, causing the attention toward these factors in others to be vital when selecting someone to build companionship with. Don't allow kindness to supersede sound judgment, friends. A story my father told me in regard to those that hurt you consistently is the story of the kangaroo and the snake.

THE KANGAROO AND THE SNAKE

Once upon a time, along the trail there hopped a joyful and kind kangaroo. Hopping along the trail on a hot, humid day, the kangaroo came across a snake that appeared to be in distress.

The snake looked up at the kangaroo and said, "Would you be able to help me out, Mr. Kangaroo? It's hot outside, I've been run over by a car, and I can't slither along how I normally do. I need your help." The snake continued, "There's a place a few miles up the road that I need to get to; could you put me in your pouch and take me?"

"Sure, why not," The kangaroo replied. So the kangaroo placed the battered snake in his pouch and started to deliver the snake where he needed to go. All of a sudden, the kangaroo felt a pinch on his stomach. "Ouch!" said the kangaroo. "You bit me!"

"Sorry," said the snake.

A few miles down the road, the kangaroo felt another uncomfortable pain in his stomach where the snake was stored inside of his pouch. "Ouch! You bit me again!" exclaimed the kangaroo.

"Sorry about that," replied the snake. The kangaroo hopped along, agitated yet still willing to transport the snake. For a third time, the kangaroo felt an alarming bite on his stomach where the snake had sunk his teeth in.

"That's it!" shouted the kangaroo. He took the snake out of his pouch and tossed him onto the ground. "Why on earth do you keep biting me?!" said the kangaroo to the snake.

The snake looked up at him and replied, "What did you expect, Mr. Kangaroo? I'm a snake—that's what I do."

When you're dealing with people, recognize snakes for what they are. It's unfortunate, but the nature of snakes can and will waste your time if you allow kindness to mask sound judgment. Though people seem trustworthy and may even be in genuine need of help, not everyone is your friend.

Also, the angry person has inner issues that manifest externally, often aimed at others in order to "unload." God says to abstain from joining with people who have addictions. A companion with an addiction is not fit for marriage. "Do not join those who drink too much wine or gorge themselves on meat, for drunkards and gluttons become poor, and drowsiness clothes them in rags" (Prv 23:20–21). Joining together with an individual who has addictions is foolish; I know this from personal experience. It is natural that you would expect to be higher than an addiction on your partner's list of priorities, but sometimes (as in the case of dating an addict) this is not the reality. Having dated a person who smoked marijuana on a daily basis, I can say that marijuana became the highest joy of her life—even greater than the stability of our relationship. She loved smoking pot so much that she would sooner give up the romantic relationship we held for weed. What a slap in the face that was! Another thing addictions create, as we all know, is dependency. Everything revolves around a dependent nature in your companion, which turns things negative very quickly. As far as the girl I dated was concerned, nothing was right when she didn't have her weed. The absence of marijuana actually sent her into panic mode. She had become so dependent on smoking before she did anything that not having it around altered her personality. She was an entirely different person.

Continuing down the line of criteria the Bible has given us, let us realize that a person with bitterness is not suitable for marriage. Hebrews says, "See to it that no one fall short of the grace of God and that no bitter root grows up to cause trouble and to defile many" (Heb 12:15). Bitterness toward your parents is not an exception. "If someone curses their father or mother, their lamp will be snuffed out in pitch darkness" (Prv 20:20). Try dating someone who is bitter about something. Often people hold grudges for past mishaps or mistreatment, whether it is from past relationships or bad parents. I dated a girl who constantly talked about how angry she was from happenings in her previous relationship. All this did was show me that she was not ready to put that behind her. A relationship with a bitter person puts an unnecessary burden on you that shouldn't have to be managed in the first place. A longtime buddy of mine from high school called me up to discuss relationships. Fed up with his results, he pledged to me over the phone that he would never date a woman with bitterness again. He referred to the particular area of bitterness he was tired of as "women with daddy issues." I asked him candidly just what he meant. "All of the women that I choose to date that don't have their fathers in their lives are a complete wreck when fathers come into conversation. They unload their bitterness on me and sometimes channel angered aggression at me like it's my fault," he said. Holding disdain for wrongs that have been done to you in the past can be natural, though what is unnatural is projecting that bitterness onto another. It makes for an unhealthy situation. Bitterness directed at parents in the form of disrespect is rebuked in the Bible, as we see in Proverbs. Disrespect toward an individual's parent from that individual is unacceptable, according to God.

Another negative trait to avoid when selecting a life partner is selfishness. "The greedy stir up conflict, but those who trust in the Lord will prosper" (Prv 28:25). "An unfriendly person pursues selfish ends and against all sound judgment starts quarrels" (Prv 18:1). While on the subject of quarrels, God warns about a quarrelsome mate, telling us that it's better to live on the roof than in a house with a quarrelsome mate (Prv 28:25). Quarrels reveal selfishness. A friend of mine recalled an instance in his past involving his parents. Reviewing the family budget, his father made it known to his mother that the budget could not support the purchase of a nice couch she had been eyeing for a month. While his father was out of town, his mother took it upon herself to go out and buy the couch anyway. His father returned home to find the couch sitting in the living room, and it immediately started a furious fight between his two parents. Selfishness sparks separation between couples. Distance between two partners in turn destroys trust. Selfishness also separates us from the most important bond we hold with Jesus Christ. The art of servant leadership (what Jesus modeled) is in opposition with selfishness. It is set up this way so that the two cannot coexist. Habitual selfishness does not lead to friendships. Relationships are important, and you cannot accumulate more friends by being selfish. The best way to gain friends is to be a friend.

Watch out for greed in a companion. "The greedy bring ruin to their households, but the one who hates bribes will live" (Prv 15:27). Again, relationships require both parties to be giving unto one another. "Do not eat the food of a begrudging host, do not crave his delicacies" (Prv 23:6). The idea of this verse is to not take what is reluctantly offered to you. Stingy people are part of this reluctant group. Inwardly they'd rather have it for themselves, so why take an artificial offer from someone? Finding a marriage candidate is an extremely important decision to make, and the reason I list God's criteria for joining with another is because as secular marriage statistics reflect, the masses are not employing these biblical standards.

My nephew is a heavy eater when he decides he's going to consume food. We'll be at my parent's house visiting when hunger strikes him, and he peruses the pantry. There have been times when he ate double and triple the amount of food he actually needed, simply because the food was available to him. Not long after he would finish, my mother would come downstairs to find that there was no bread left! Next thing you know, my nephew is getting taught a lesson on greed due to his lack of self-control. My nephew's situation is written off as an understandable, even cute occurrence when it happens. In the grown-up world of dating to find your life partner, greediness is not as cute. In fact there have been many cases where a husband or wife has financially devastated his or her family. An example of this that I can recall is the greed in gambling. One of the two spouses consistently gambles away the bill money, expecting to win on his or her bets, of course. Greed comes in all shapes and sizes. Do not be fooled or become entangled with someone who keeps greed in his or her repertoire.

Last but definitely not least of the God-ordained instruction for choosing a mate is to pick a mate who is generous and kind. "A generous man will prosper; whoever refreshes others will be refreshed" (Prv 11:25). Pick people up when they are down, and you will find that they will in turn pick you up when you are down. I personally decided to implement this wisdom on a small scale at work. One way to convey generosity was buying my partner dinner for the night. Working twenty-four hour shifts as a paramedic with a partner means going through all three meals with one another. I decided to purchase my partner's dinner one night, and the joy he conveyed brought me a refreshing feeling. I noticed a change in his demeanor that shift, a change toward a happier demeanor. Another way I chose to be generous was making a heightened effort in taking on station chores. Dishes needed to be washed, the microwave needed cleaning, our ambulance wasn't the cleanest, and more. Since my partner was tied up on the computer getting other things done, I eased out to the areas where chores needed to be completed. My result was again an attitude of gratitude from my partner, which left me refreshed. On a separate day, he returned the favor, which refreshed me!

In the dating world, the art of generosity will take you everywhere. Memorable accounts of when I really sprang to be more generous than usual were the times my dates had the most fun. They would express to me how much fun they had, and I have a confident feeling that it was an amplified time of fun for them because I made it all about *them*. People cherish the generosity you extend them. We also find that generosity is reflected as other great traits when looked at by other people. What I mean is that generosity makes people comfortable with you, comfortable enough to tell you more things that they may normally hold in from timidity. Listen, readers, especially those of you who are not yet married: I cannot emphasize how concrete scripture is for choosing a partner in marriage. I've dated plenty of women and have done so without any direction or criteria. I also know plenty of female friends who have done the same. God knows what we truly desire in our hearts, and if you're truly serious about finding the woman or man of your dreams, all you have to do is trust in your Creator. He designed you, and therefore he knows you better than you know yourself. Proverbs 31 spells out a woman of God. The book of Ruth is a great example for the kind of man God would want a godly woman to have. Don't compromise long-term satisfaction for a cheap thrill or stolen moment. Make sure the man or woman you seek is God's selection. Wasting time wearies your soul. Misdirected effort is tiring, even to the physical body. It's like a boxer who throws a haymaker and misses. Focusing your efforts in the God-approved areas with God-approved criteria for searching will yield the Lord's blessings.

Run away from sexual immorality as much as you can because it is a trap. When you have multiple sex partners, you build soul ties with individuals that ought not to have soul ties with you. God wanted a soul tie to be made with your spouse because deep emotions are attached, and he knew how powerful it is to have soul ties outside of marriage. Joseph gave us a great example of what action to take in the face of sexual temptation—*run!* Joseph did nothing but run. Preserve your deep romantic feelings for your wife or your husband, where true love was meant to be fostered. God rewards those who wait patiently. When you wait, you won't have to compromise. Compromising on such a sacred thing as marriage is for fools and fools alone. God left us the blueprints for marriage, so my advice to you derived from personal failures and studying the Bible is to *use them!*

CHAPTER 10
SPIRIT OF JEZEBEL

I'D LIKE THE READER TO know of a spiritual war that is beyond the naked eye. It's an ancient war that has been going on for years and years that must be addressed, for it is more powerful than any battle I've ever fought. I'm convinced that this is the most powerful, most difficult battle that I will ever fight. I dealt with the spirit of Jezebel one-on-one for a few years, unaware of what it was and that it even existed. Being ignorant and unknowledgeable of what I was facing facilitated a further fall down the slippery slope of sexual seduction and sin. Please open your hearts to the information I'm about to share with you, for the Jezebel spirit is like quicksand; by the time you are in it, only an outside strength (God) can pull you out of that hole. My goal is that you can properly identify this well-disguised pool of quicksand and take an alternate route. I, unfortunately, was too uninformed, arrogant, and above all willing to roll the dice with a force such as this.

Though this spirit came from a woman in the Bible, we should not make the mistake of thinking it does not or cannot manifest itself in men as its host. As an avid competitor, I believe a valuable measure to take when battling is to know your opponent; this way the disguises and techniques your opponents use will not obliterate your efforts. So we will start out reviewing just who Jezebel is, what her attributes are, and how she operates.

Jezebel is first introduced in the book of 1 Kings when an evil king named Ahab took her to be his wife: "He not only considered it trivial to commit the sins of Jeroboam son of Nabat, but he also married Jezebel daughter of Ethbaal king of the Sidonians, and began to serve Baal and worship him" (1 Kgs 16:31). To give you an idea of just how evil King Ahab was, the Bible says in 1 Kings 16:33 that Ahab did more to provoke God's anger than did all the kings of Israel before him! Queen Jezebel hated the Lord's prophets; in fact she killed them off as she so desired: "While Jezebel was killing off the Lord's prophets, Obadiah had taken one hundred prophets and hidden them into caves, fifty in each, and had supplied them with food and water" (1 Kgs 18:4). By this Bible verse alone, you can conclude that Jezebel was an evil murderer who was in full opposition to God. The mighty prophet Elijah heard of this from Obadiah and was led by the Lord to announce his presence to King Ahab. Elijah summoned the prophets of Baal and the four hundred prophets of Asherah who ate at Jezebel's table. Elijah called these wicked prophets for a showdown on Mount Carmel. Two bulls were chosen to be sacrificed, one by each side, and each side agreed to pray to its god and ask for fire to burn the sacrifice. Whichever god answered would be considered true. Elijah was triumphant in the showdown, and even taunted the false prophets when their bull sacrifice did not catch on fire! Elijah had the prophets brought down Kishon Valley to be slaughtered; this infuriated Jezebel. When Jezebel heard of this, she pledged that Elijah's destiny would be just the same as her prophets' destiny: death. Elijah fled to Mount Horeb for his life.

Jezebel also forged a letter in the name of her husband, King Ahab, to have Naboth killed for his vineyard. What spawned this evil act of murder was Naboth rejecting King Ahab's offer to buy his vineyard. King Ahab behaved like a child upon the rejection by going to his bed and refusing to eat. Elijah returned to give Ahab a message from the Lord. His message was that because Ahab provoked the Lord to anger, the Lord would lessen his estate, and as for Jezebel, dogs would devour her by the wall of Jezreel.

I've compiled a list of Jezebel's character traits that are backed by Bible verses. Many have sensationalized Jezebel by providing information about the spirit that is often the result of speculation. The points I shall cover have been dissected by scripture and scripture only, and you will find that they are blatantly detectable once you are equipped with the knowledge of what to look for:

1. Hate for the Lord's Prophets
2. Infliction of Fear
3. Manipulation and Lies
4. Attraction to Weak Men
5. Licentiousness
6. Lewd Adornment
7. Unwillingness to Repent
8. Toleration
9. Embedment in the Media

HATE FOR THE LORD'S PROPHETS

The first trait this spirit holds is a disgust and hatred for the Lord's prophets. "Jezebel was killing off the Lord's prophets" is what 1 Kings says in 18:4. Jezebel sent a death threat to the prophet Elijah via a messenger that read, "May the gods deal with me, be it ever so severely, if by this time tomorrow I do not make your life like that of one of them" (1 Kgs 19:2). As I previously informed you, what she was referring to when saying *them* was all of the prophets of hers that Elijah had slaughtered. He killed her prophets, so she vowed to return the favor by killing Elijah.

INFLICTION OF FEAR

An illustration of just how much power the spirit of Jezebel contains is marked by the ability to inflict fear: "Elijah was afraid and ran for his life. When he came to Beersheba and Judah, he left his servant there, while he himself went a day's journey into the desert. He came to a broom tree, sat down under it and prayed that he might die. I have had enough, Lord, he said. Take my life; I am no better than my ancestors" (1 Kgs 19:3–4). Let's take a time-out and give this some thought. We're not talking about any old weak-kneed young fellow who wets the bed and is still afraid of the dark. Elijah was a prophet from God! A great one! Elijah parted the Jordan River through the power of God. Elijah struck down a captain and fifty men three different times with fire while praying on a hill. This is the same mighty prophet who had the showdown on Mount Carmel, talking trash and taunting the false prophets as he strove toward a great victory. I can just imagine him strutting around like a barnyard rooster up on Mount Carmel with the neck action and everything! And then it is revealed that Jezebel has such a mighty prophet on the run, so afraid that he asked God to take his life. Talk about stress. I can assure you that this particular spirit is a force to reckon with indeed. Only the power of God can deliver you from its evil strongholds.

MANIPULATION AND LIES

Manipulative methods intertwined with lies are part of the twisted makeup of Jezebel. There's proof of this in the tactics she takes in gaining Naboth's vineyard. "So she wrote letters in Ahab's name, placed *his* seal on them, and sent them to the elders and nobles who lived in Naboth's city with him. In those letters she wrote: proclaim a day of fasting and seek Naboth in a prominent place among the people. But seat two scoundrels opposite him and have them testify that he has cursed both God and the king. Then take him out and stone him to death" (1 Kgs 21:8–10, emphasis mine). Manipulative nature strongly indicates a Jezebel spirit. Dating or being married to someone with these attributes makes for misery. Lies, which work hand in hand with manipulation, cause terrible disagreements, giving birth to trust issues in a relationship. Avoid this spirit at all costs when faced with it; you will save yourself an abundance of both anger and grief. Profound, unspeakable grief stems from allowing the spirit to fester in your life. It is a selfish, self-directed, self-interested spirit that does not promote a godly relationship.

ATTRACTION TO WEAK MEN

Jezebel was attracted to a weak man. Spineless men don't stand a chance against this spirit. Chapter 21 of 1 Kings illustrates how weak of a man Jezebel likes.

So Ahab went home, sullen and angry because Naboth the Jezreelite had said, I will not give you the inheritance of my fathers. He lay on his bed sulking and refused to eat. His wife Jezebel came in and asked him, why are you so sullen? Why won't you eat? He answered, because I said to Naboth the Jezreelite, sell me your vineyard; or if you prefer, I will give you another vineyard in its place. But he said, I will not give you my vineyard. Jezebel his wife said, is this how you act as the king over Israel? Get up and eat! Cheer up. I'll get you the vineyard of Naboth the Jezreelite. (1 Kgs 21:4–7)

What kind of man goes to his bedroom to pout and whine like a child, refusing to eat? A weak-spirited man; a weak-spirited man is exactly what King Ahab was. A true woman would be ashamed of a man (in this case a king) who sulks over not getting his way. The way Ahab cries is reflective of a toddler not getting his way. A weak man fits into the framework of someone like Queen Jezebel because she would be the dominant one in the relationship. A relationship with a passive, weak-backed man such as King Ahab is the exact habitat for manipulation and lies to flourish in. Passiveness only builds strength in a person like Jezebel because what weakens a strong-willed person of evil deeds such as her is a cessation initiated by an opposing force. How much of an opposing force do you think King Ahab was when he was the kind of man to throw an immature fit over spilled milk?

Work to not be passive under such manipulative forces. The more time spent adhering to a passive complex, the easier it is to remain weak and passive. Christian men are charged with the responsibility of being the head of the household, according to

Ephesians 5:23. But that is not to omit our charge of treating our wives with the same measure of love Christ did the church. The role of a Christian wife is to submit to her husband in everything, according to Ephesians 5:24. Proof of Jezebel's manipulative nature reveals itself through verse 25 in 1 Kings chapter 21: "There was never a man like Ahab, who sold himself to do evil in the eyes of the Lord, *urged on* by Jezebel his wife" (emphasis mine). She supported Ahab's evil ways, having a hand in it by urging him on.

LICENTIOUSNESS

Jezebel was a licentious female. In the book of Revelation, God rebukes such behavior: "By her teachings she misleads my servants into sexual immorality and the eating of food sacrificed to idols" (Rv 2:20). Licentiousness is defined as "sexually unrestrained." A sexually unrestrained woman is the absolute last burden a man should have to bear. Being sexually unrestrained leads to adultery, which God despises with a passion: "My son, give me your heart and let your eyes keep to my ways, for a prostitute is a deep pit and a wayward wife is a narrow well. Like a bandit she waits and multiplies the unfaithful among men" (Prv 23:26–28). Try being at work accompanied by the agonal thoughts of adultery taking place behind your back; it's not fun. As a matter of fact, it has the ability to drive you mad. I've been in such situations where I was wondering profusely, questioning my other half's integrity. God gives us sound advice for decoding an unfaithful mate in Proverbs: "This is the way of an adulteress; she eats and wipes her mouth and says, 'I've done nothing wrong'" (Prv 30:20). What this particular verse conveys is a lack of humility. Humility displays godly character. Humility is the essence of repentance! Since it is my deep concern for the masses to comprehend the importance of this subject, I shall continue unraveling what God has to say about adultery because it's such a large issue in the world. God says in Proverbs 7:27 that the adulterous woman's house is a highway to the grave, leading down to the chambers of death. Chapter 7 in Proverbs serves as a genuine warning against the adulterous. I take the time to extend such candid information because my desire is to extend sound wisdom to you so that the troubling terrors I have endured do not beset you. I've seen ugliness. Ugliness only a dark, twisted nightmare could conceive. Chapter 5 of Proverbs is another chapter solely dedicated to warning against adultery. To the men, I extend to you with love, "Do not spend your strength on women, your vigor on those who ruin kings" (Prv 31:3–4). And to the women, I also extend the same warning concerning an adulterer; this is not God's plan for you. Licentiousness drowns out the wisdom of the Lord. Solomon got so deep into sexual immorality that he ended up losing track of what he believed. He somehow forgot that it was the Lord who endowed him with godly wisdom, forgetfulness which resulted in the worship of a pagan god. Retribution inevitably takes place for sinning against the Lord. God tore Solomon's kingdom away from him: "Although he had forbidden Solomon to follow other gods, Solomon did not keep the Lord's command. So the Lord said to Solomon, since this is your attitude and you have not kept my covenant and my decrees, which I commanded you, I will most certainly tear the kingdom away from you and give it to one of your subordinates" (1 Kgs 11:10–11). The word of the Lord toward Jezebel's sexual lewdness was to lay her on a bed of suffering, and God said he would kill her children.

God killed David's firstborn child with Bathsheba because the child was conceived through both adultery and the murder of Bathsheba's husband. Licentiousness that resulted in death is mentioned in the book of Numbers: "Then an Israelite man brought into the camp a Midianite woman right before the eyes of Moses and the whole assembly of Israel while they were weeping at the entrance to the tent of meeting. When Phinehas son of Eleazar, the son of Aaron, the priest, saw this, he left the assembly, took a spear in his hand and followed the Israelite into the tent. He drove the spear into both of them, right through the Israelite man and into the woman's stomach. Then the plague against the Israelites was stopped" (Nm 25:8). A buddy of mine *died* going to see about a woman around 4:00 a.m. She fooled him and was waiting with a shotgun, along with her boyfriend, when he arrived. He was beaten to death with that very shotgun, having his wallet stolen as well as his car. Licentiousness has no place in the sight of the Lord. Digest my sincerest warning. Trust me, if anyone knows the struggle of sexual sin, it would be me. To everyone's fortune, however, God has provided a venue to operate in sexually. Marriage is the God ordained arena sexuality is permitted to thrive in.

LEWD ADORNMENT

"Then Jehu went to Jezreel. When Jezebel heard about it, she painted her eyes, arranged her hair and looked out of the window. As Jehu entered the gate, she asked, have you come in peace, Zimri, you murderer of your master?" (2 Kgs 9:30–31). Misdirection through beauty and adornment is a key characteristic that mirrors a Jezebel spirit. Beauty just may be the greatest tool to mislead a man. To thwart such measures by the Jezebel spirit, we must train our eyes to see the person's actions instead of beautification or a smooth tongue. Notice how she made herself all pretty and spoke with sweetness, even up until her bitter end was just about to take place. Beauty is vain, according to the Bible. Beauty can be admirable, but it has an expiration date on it—it is fleeting. And in evil situations such as this, beauty works diligently to redirect focus. King Jehu came to kill Jezebel, and her attempt at illusive beautification failed. Samson became unfocused when he revealed the secret to his strength to Delilah. Solomon lost focus when he left God to follow the pagan idols of his many wives. Can you see the dots I'm trying to connect for you? Stay focused.

I'd like to leave with you two gems I've learned to guard against the deceptive advances of a Jezebel spirit. The first gem comes from Matthew: "Watch out for false prophets. They come to you in sheep's clothing, but inwardly they are ferocious wolves. By their fruit you will recognize them. Do people pick grapes from thorn bushes, or figs from thistles? Likewise, every good tree bears good fruit, but a bad tree bears bad fruit" (Mt 7:15–17). Distracting beauty cannot change a person's fruit. All you have to pay attention to is a person's fruit to recognize who they are. Proverbs says that the lips of an adulterous woman drip honey and her words are smoother than oil. Like they tell you in baseball, "keep your eye on the ball"; you must discipline yourself to keep your eye on the fruit. Jezebel called herself a prophetess, clearly following false idols such as Baal and Asherah. She also was a serial murderer. So she definitely bore rotten fruit, not fruit of the Spirit.

The second gem is found in Proverb 31, the chapter dedicated to outlining a wife of noble character: "She speaks with wisdom and faithful instruction is on her tongue" (Prv 31:26). I list this verse because it clearly states the way a righteous woman speaks. Listen to the words a person uses, and keep in mind that Proverbs tells us that "charm is deceptive" in 31:30. These two gems should help filter the misleading and deviant tactics adornment employs in both beautification and speech.

Unwillingness To Repent

"I have given her time to repent of her immorality and she is unwilling" (Rv 2:21). This character flaw in the Jezebel spirit is flagrant and overt. God hates an unrepentant spirit because this lack of humility and arrogance locks individuals out of heaven! Without repentance, there is no forgiveness of sins or the extension of merciful grace from God, which none of us can live without! When I learned of this unwillingness to repent in my ex-girlfriend of almost three years, it only added to the tears I cried. There was no amount of convincing that could be done because her self-righteousness drowned out any righteous reasoning. Be aware of this particular attribute; you won't have to conduct an investigation to find it. Jezebel did not hide it, and neither will a person you may interface with. What Christians must do is maintain Christlike character in our patience and pray for these individuals.

Toleration

"Nevertheless, I have this against you: You *tolerate* that woman Jezebel, who calls herself a prophetess" (Rv 2:20, emphasis mine). Notice the word God uses when addressing the church of Thyatira: *tolerate*. The implication of having a choice is made in this verse, meaning it is our decision as believers to allow such a spirit to continue on in our presence. Many angles of this spirit appear to be intriguing to a person who is wrapped up in the illusion the Jezebel spirit offers. It's like a multifaceted diamond rotating on a glass-enclosed jewelry stand. I've been in the thick of being enthralled by the gaudy glamour the spirit of Jezebel eludes; it's *entrancing*. So entrancing it will make you forget who you are, what you stand for, and how you wandered so far down this rabbit hole to begin with. Let me tell you something about this evil spirit: if you recognize it, your best bet is to get out of there—plain and simple. Don't try and reason your way through by way of philosophical arguments in your head. Time is of the essence, and by the way, time is not on your side in this particular matter.

Probably the most convicting sermon I've ever attended was in my hometown. My pastor spoke on this topic, executing with poise and potency. His posture was upright as he slowly looked up from his notes on the podium, peering through his reading glasses at the congregation sitting out in the pews. He took two steps back, briefly pausing before he said, "You tolerate that woman, Jezebel...You *tolerate* that woman, Jezebel." Taking a stand against this spirit is not passive; it does not allow finesse to bring its advances to a halt. The only thing passive in regard to this ancient spirit is the toleration of it. Just as King Jehu was assertive in squelching this evil, you must also take the same approach, not the week-kneed, passive approach illustrated by King Ahab.

EMBEDMENT IN THE MEDIA

Our media depicts this spirit everywhere: in sales ads, movies, commercials, sitcoms, books, radio, and the Internet. Like many repetitive exposures do in the media, a brainwashing or sedative effect intercedes in our minds, desensitizing believers to red flags and caution signs. What's worse is that when you don't even know what you're looking for, you have a zero probability of finding those Jezebel qualities. Wake up and rebel against these repetitious attempts at injecting nonsense into your brain. If you read any popular magazine, it won't take you long to find the sections that claim to have so-called secrets of beauty and success. Without fail, they always seem to point toward external appearances. Such superficial measures are in contrast with true doctrine from the Holy Bible. God cares about character and nobility; he hates haughty eyes and a proud look. Open up the Bible, and you will find that the lies told in self-help books and fashion magazines are mere hoaxes. Every now and then, an app will pop up on my phone. A new app being promoted is called Covet Fashion. The irony in the title of this "must-have" phone app is comical in and of itself. To covet fashion means to wrongfully desire fashion. Most individuals playing these phone app games wouldn't take time to look up words in front of them that they don't know, and so the joke is on them. Maintain awareness, stay in the Word of God, and ask for a cloak of protection when you pray. Spiritual protection is needed; therefore you may as well utilize the most powerful form of defense you have as a believer—which is God.

CHAPTER 11

SIGN NUMBER THREE

DURING ALL OF THE TURMOIL I endured in 2014 with the loss of my job, my romantic love life, and my vehicle, God showed me a total of three signs of his presence in my life as a response to fervent prayer and pleading with him. Two of these three amazing signs I have covered previously in this text: the *cross in the corner* I saw after praying for God to show me he was "in my corner" at work and a dream he spoke to me through in the form of *two vocabulary words* I had not known prior to this dream. On both of these occasions, I asked the Lord to show me a sign marked by evidence that it was from the Lord and not my own mental shenanigans.

This third sign I experienced resonates with me the strongest because it is a sign others have shared in numerous accounts throughout the Bible. It's embroidered in the fabric of the lives of multiple biblical figures. Sign number three was going through a forty-day testing period, which I recognized thanks to keeping time-stamped journal entries in my personal prayer book. Documenting my prayers revealed to me that going through renewal from the wreckage of my life and toleration of the Jezebel spirit resulted in a forty-day period. It was undoubtedly a transformation period. Specifically, my depression-induced weakness spanned from the day my ex-girlfriend left my apartment to the first day of my new job. Interestingly enough, my start date at my new job was originally seven days sooner, and they pushed it back a week. In hindsight, I can clearly see that this was the mighty hand of God allotting enough time for the transformation to run its course. When God assigns a transformation, it is for his purposes. Today, you are reading a result of the forty day transformation he assigned to *me* for his purposes. I've never been one to expose such personal matters, but here I am crucifying myself (figuratively, not literally) in order to strengthen your faith. The Lord knew both my physical condition and my mental condition required every bit of that forty-day period. The truth is that the three years or so I invested in my relationship broke me down. A woman I had planned to spend the rest of my life with was now gone. So instead of starting my job when originally scheduled, God extended my time so I could regain enough strength to properly function. My depression exceeded these forty days, but my ability to focus and perform effectively returned to me.

To give clarity on the number of times *forty* is mentioned in the Bible, let's review:

- The rains fell for forty days and nights (Gn 7:4)
- Israel ate manna for forty days (Ex 16:35)
- Moses was with God on Mount Sinai for forty days and nights (Ex 24:18)
- Moses was again with God forty days and nights (Exodus 34:28)

- The spies searched the land of Canaan for forty days (Nm 13:25)
- God made Israel wander for forty years (Nm 14:33–34)
- Forty stripes was the maximum whipping penalty (Dt 25:3)
- God allowed the land to rest for forty years (Judges 3:11, 5:31, 8:28)
- Abdon—a judge in Israel—had forty sons (Jgs 12:14)
- Israel did evil; God gave them to an enemy forty years (Jgs 13:1)
- Eli judged Israel for forty years (1 Sm 4:18)
- Goliath presented himself for forty days (1 Sm 17:16)
- Saul reigned for forty years (Acts 13:21)
- Ishbosheth—Saul's son—was forty when he began his reign (2 Sm 2:10)
- David reigned over Israel for forty years (2 Sm 5:14, 1 Kgs 2:11)
- The holy place of the temple was forty cubits long (1 Kgs 6:17)
- Forty baths (a measurement) was the size of the lavers in the temple (1 Kgs 7:38)
- The sockets of silver are in groups of forty (Ex 26:19, 21)
- Solomon reigned forty years like his father David (1 Kgs 11:42)
- Elijah had one meal that sustained him for forty days (1 Kgs 19:8)
- Ezekiel bore the iniquity of the house of Judah for forty days (Ez 4:6)
- Jehoash—starting at seven years old—reigned forty years in Jerusalem (2 Kgs 12:1)
- Egypt was to be laid desolate for forty years (Ez 29:11–12)
- Ezekiel's symbolic temple is forty cubits long (Ez 41:2)

- The courts in Ezekiel's temple were forty cubits long (Ezr 46:22)
- God gave Nineveh forty days to repent (Jon 3:4)
- Jesus fasted forty days and nights (Mt 4:2)
- Jesus was tempted forty days (Lk 4:2, Mk 1:13)
- Jesus remained on earth forty days after resurrection (Acts 1:3)

This is not a full list; there are more instances than those recorded in this book. But the reader can clearly see how frequently forty is mentioned and its apparent significance of transformation. Moses created the Ten Commandments in this timeframe! As a paramedic, I find it also relative to mention that women have a forty-week gestational period before giving birth. Think about how much of a testing period pregnancies are for women. And undeniably, pregnancies are a transformation period; if you can't see it, just look at the transformation a woman's stomach undergoes over the forty-week period! I also found it interesting how the prophet Elijah fled into the wilderness and traveled forty days and nights when faced with Jezebel—the same spirit I dealt with just before my forty-day period of transformation surfaced.

I encourage believers to pay close attention to what God may be showing you in each of your lives. I also encourage you to think highly enough of God to request his presence be revealed in your life. Prayers work effectively, but it takes wholehearted *action* to have your prayers considered. Let us pray. "Dear Lord, we come to you in Jesus Christ's undaunted and holy name asking for strength. Lord, we ask that you shed mercy on our lives as we learn of your sovereign power. Help each of us to linger in the safety of your protection. Help us to be thankful in the times of struggle just as much as we are thankful in the times of prosperity. We ask that you show us your mighty hand at work in our lives so that we may speak with even more enthusiasm of your holy righteousness through testimonies. Give each of us what we need to sustain ourselves just as you sustained Elijah for forty days off of one meal. You are a pure and amazing God. We are faithfully your servants, and though we stumble, our salvation cannot be taken from us. Guide us to greener pastures and higher spiritual maturity. In your son Jesus's name, we pray. Amen."

CHAPTER 12

WALK WITH A LIMP

A MEDICAL STORY

The most prevalent emergency call paramedics respond to in Florida, a state saturated with elderly people who have come to Florida to retire, is falls. Not falls from building tops, palm trees, or ladders; just regular ground-level falls. There are slips and falls. There are trips and falls. There are sudden-weakness falls. There are syncopal falls (fainting). There are roll-out-of-bed falls. There are psychiatric patients who *believe* they are falling. Everyone seems to be falling where I come from. An outcome of a little old lady or man who has fallen can sometimes be a broken hip. A broken hip causes a great deal of pain in an older person—and in anyone, for that matter. We paramedics go through a series of precautionary measures before we even move the patient, who more often than not is lying on his or her back or side in immense pain. We use a pain scale to get an idea of how bad the patient's pain is by asking, "How bad is your pain on a scale of one to ten, with ten being the worst pain you've ever felt in your entire life?" Every so often you get the overly distressed patient who shouts, "My pain is a fifteen out of ten!" Anyway, we use what's called a scoop stretcher, which is a backboard that can be separated into two halves down the middle to make placing the patient with a hip injury easier. Another preventative measure paramedics initiate is the administration of narcotic analgesics, or pain meds. Administering pain medication prior to moving the patient does the patient a huge favor in helping to deal with the pain from the injury. Whether it be morphine, fentanyl, dilaudid, or another drug, our narcotic analgesics do a great job at inducing a higher threshold for pain. An outcome that narcotic analgesics do not prevent is a musculoskeletal imbalance known as *shortening*. Shortening is a result of having a broken or fractured hip, making one leg shorter than the other. Since one leg is shorter than the other, this particular person winds up inadvertently walking with a limp. Nothing is wrong with it; it's actually very commendable that a person presses on after such an injury, even if it is with a walker or cane. It shows tenacity. It shows perseverance. It shows courage and strength. Christians may find themselves doing the same thing, only in their spiritual walk.

Take Jacob into account. Jacob wrestled with God and came out with an injured hip after God touched his hip:

When the man saw that he could not overpower him, he touched at the socket of Jacob's hip that his hip was wrenched as he wrestled with the man. The man said, let me go, for it is daybreak. But Jacob replied, I will not let you go until you bless me. The man asked him, what is your name? Jacob answered. Then the man said, your name will no longer be Jacob, but Israel, because you have struggled with God and with humans and have overcome. Jacob said, please tell me your name. But he replied, why do you ask my name? Then he blessed him there. So Jacob called the place Peniel, saying it is because I saw God face-to-face, and yet my life was spared. The sun rose above him as he passed Peniel, and he was *limping* because of his hip. (Gn 32:25–31, emphasis mine)

Jacob had a great intention of receiving a blessing from God, which is what each of us should possess. An additional model of having to walk with a limp is Paul: "Therefore, in order to keep me from becoming conceited, I was given a thorn in my flesh, a messenger of Satan, to torment me" (2 Cor 12:7). Paul rejoiced in having this thorn in his side because weaknesses mean strength in Christ.

Growing up, I met a wonderful lady who lived across the street from my parents' house who today I call my grandmother. Our relationship began when I began cutting her grass and watching her dog during her annual cruises in January. My duty was to make sure her dog, Nikki, was fed and let outside at the scheduled times she left me. We grew our bond through challenging puzzles as well as games such as Yahtzee and Scrabble. She was a reader. She dedicated an entire room to serve as a personal library. The amount of books she read would knock your socks off. She has children and was once married.

Our visits lessened as I got older, but one visit I made to my grandmother opened up the door of discussion that revealed a mutual challenge, or limp. We sat one night on her plush white leather sectional sofa chatting it up late into the evening. I told her of the way things were coming together in my life in the Lord, and she updated me on her endeavors. She explained to me of how even today, her ex-husband brings up her name unnecessarily in a negative or manipulative way. She expressed to me that she could not understand for the life of her why he would do these things. Hoping to console my adopted grandmother, I told her to fret not and think of me as a spiritual partner who aches in very much the same way—and I do. Even today—just as my adopted grandmother is reminded of the limp that she has incurred from her past—I too walk with that same, familiar limp. In one way or another, I am reminded of the devastation I have incurred from my past experiences. Walking with a limp is an honor given to us from God. It helps us to remember who we are and how we got to where we are currently. Nothing but the blood of Jesus and God's grace have placed those who believe where they are. My limp that I walk with is my broken heart; what's your limp? "The sacrifices of God are a broken spirit; a broken and contrite heart, O God, you will not despise" (Ps 51:17). If either a broken heart or depression ails you at this point in time, cling to the Lord, and he shall deliver you—I promise. Let this passage be your battle cry: "Hear my prayer, oh Lord, listen to my cry for help; be not deaf to my weeping. For I dwell with you as an alien, a stranger, as all my fathers were. Look away from me, that I may rejoice again before I depart and am no more" (Ps 39:12–13). "I waited patiently for the Lord; he turned to me and heard my cry. He lifted me out of the slimy pit, out of the mud and mire; he set my feet on a rock and gave me a firm place to stand. He put a new song in my mouth, a hymn of praise to our God. Many will see and fear and put their trust in the Lord. Blessed is the man [or woman] who makes the Lord his trust, who does not look to the proud, to those who turn aside to false gods" (Ps 40:1–4). It is not out of the ordinary for a believer in Christ to walk with baggage. It is not uncommon for a believer in God to struggle onward as he or she walks with a limp. You are not alone in the challenge to press on. Maybe you're not in a position where your heart has been broken. Maybe there is another test of time known only to you that you keep internalized. Whatever your individual case may be, place your problems and pains in God's lap; that's what he's here for. God never expected us to wield the sword all on our own. King David brought about all sorts of problems on his family when he committed his sin. Samson ended up blind. Ezekiel lost his wife. Daniel was thrown into a den of roaring lions. Joseph was hated by his own family. Paul suffered many things:

> I have worked much harder, been in prison more frequently, been flogged more severely and been exposed to death again and again. Five times I received from the Jews the forty lashes minus one. Three times I was beaten with rods, once I was stoned, three times I was shipwrecked, I spent a night and a day in the open sea, I have been constantly on the move. I've been in danger from rivers, in danger from bandits, in danger from my own countrymen, in danger from Gentiles; in danger in the city, in danger in the country, in danger at sea; and in danger from false brothers. I have labored and toiled and have often gone without sleep; I have known hunger and thirst and have often gone without food; I've been cold and naked. Besides everything else, I face daily the pressure of my concern for all the churches. Who is

weak, and I do not feel weak? Who is led into sin, and I
do not inwardly burn? (2 Cor 11:23–29)

Tests only strengthen those who believe. What is the size of
your faith? Do you run and hide in the face of adversity? God is
looking for tenacious warriors willing to walk up the stairway
to heaven, even if it means doing so with a limp. But before the
shining light of that stairway comes into full view, you must de-
pend on God to succeed in the trenches of the corridor leading
up to that stairway. Do not lose hope, and do not concede defeat
when life turns you upside down. Lean on God's power, and he
shall aid you in all things.

Made in the USA
Charleston, SC
09 August 2015